New Directions for
Student Services

John H. Schuh
EDITOR-IN-CHIEF

Elizabeth J. Whitt
ASSOCIATE EDITOR

Developing
Social Justice Allies

Robert D. Reason
Ellen M. Broido
Tracy L. Davis
Nancy J. Evans
EDITORS

Number 110 • Summer 2005
Jossey-Bass
San Francisco

DEVELOPING SOCIAL JUSTICE ALLIES
Robert D. Reason, Ellen M. Broido, Tracy L. Davis, Nancy J. Evans (eds.)
New Directions for Student Services, no. 110
John H. Schuh, Editor-in-Chief
Elizabeth J. Whitt, Associate Editor

NEW DIRECTIONS FOR STUDENT SERVICES (ISSN 0164-7970, e-ISSN 1536-
0695) is part of The Jossey-Bass Higher and Adult Education Series and
is published quarterly by Wiley Subscription Services, Inc., A Wiley Com-
pany, at Jossey-Bass, 989 Market Street, San Francisco, California 94103-
1741. Periodicals Postage Paid at San Francisco, California, and at
additional mailing offices. POSTMASTER: Send address changes to New
Directions for Student Services, Jossey-Bass, 989 Market Street, San Francisco, California 94103-1741.

New Directions for Student Services is indexed in College Student Personnel Abstracts and Contents Pages in Education.

Microfilm copies of issues and articles are available in 16mm and 35mm,
as well as microfiche in 105mm, through University Microfilms Inc., 300
North Zeeb Road, Ann Arbor, Michigan 48106-1346.

SUBSCRIPTIONS cost $75 for individuals and $170 for institutions, agencies,
and libraries. See ordering information page at end of book.

EDITORIAL CORRESPONDENCE should be sent to the Editor-in-Chief,
John H. Schuh, N 243 Lagomarcino Hall, Iowa State University, Ames,
Iowa 50011.

www.josseybass.com

CONTENTS

EDITORS' NOTES

The fiftieth anniversary of the *Brown v. Board of Education* decision (1954) called us as student affairs professionals to reconsider and reaffirm our commitment to social justice. It is a time to articulate, to both ourselves and the constituencies we serve (first and foremost, although not exclusively, our students) why we do social justice work. It is also important to articulate what right we have to do this work, especially in the light of a renewed call for higher education to stick to subject content and avoid politically controversial topics (Fish, 2004; Horowitz, 2004). Critics may ask if we are imposing our values (we are), say that we promote conformity with a single way of thought (we do not), and argue that we are appropriating the issues and voices of social groups to which we may not belong (we try very hard not to).

No one has yet made the case that student affairs professionals have come out primarily on the side of social justice and civil rights, and there is ample historical evidence of times that individual student affairs practitioners acted (and continue to act) to reinforce oppression. However, we also have a history of philosophical commitment to social justice dating from the second Student Personnel Point of View and reflected in the current mission statements of the American College Personnel Association and the National Association of Student Personnel Administrators (Evans and Reason, 2001), and there exists evidence of student affairs workers' addressing racial prejudice as early as the 1920s (Wolf-Wendel and others, 2004). We hope this volume builds on this history and these values, serving not as another philosophical statement but as a call to action.

Allies have action-oriented identities and must negotiate complex roles. In some respects, they have their feet in the worlds of both the dominant and the oppressed. They need to continually and accurately judge when it is most appropriate and effective for them to listen, to speak up, or to absent themselves from the discussion. They share the struggle to end oppression without sharing the oppression. They have the privileges of dominant group membership and are suspect members because of their ally work. They may choose to forgo a few aspects of their privilege, but most cannot be waived. They must speak *with* the oppressed without speaking *for* the oppressed.

Allies must struggle to answer the question, "What right do I have to do this work?" Although there is no single answer, it is important that all people working as social justice allies develop their own answers based on their histories and identities. We as the editors and the chapter authors bring our own histories and identities to our work on social justice issues, particularly to our work as allies. Among us, we have a mix of dominant and target identities, but we share a commitment to make college campuses places where all community members are respected, validated, and fostered in developing their full potential. We present this volume to assist us all in finding our answers. It is our intention to encourage the development of ally attitudes and action in both our students and our student affairs colleagues. We encourage you to use the strategies presented in the following chapters not only to encourage student growth but also as a catalyst to reconsider and reaffirm your own commitment to social justice work.

In Chapters One and Two, we present the conceptual foundation for social justice ally development. These chapters serve as the common literature base on which the subsequent chapters are built. Chapters Three through Seven present strategies for the development of social justice behaviors in specific dominant group members. In each case, we have intentionally enlisted voices of authors who identify with the dominant and target groups on which the chapter focuses. Not only do we hope to model the cross-identity collaboration we encourage in this book, but we believe the inclusion of multiple voices enriches the discussion in each chapter. Just as we bring our own social identities to these chapters, we also bring areas of professional expertise and passion; thus, we acknowledge that this volume does not address all forms of oppression. Rather, we offer it as the next addition to the continued exploration of power, privilege, and oppression. Finally, although we present the chapters as distinct units, we recognize that any single individual will identify with multiple identities—both dominant and target group identities.

We hope that this volume inspires you to action. We understand that translating this text into action presents the most difficult, and frightening, step of the ally development process, so we leave you with the words of Parker Palmer, an educational activist and writer who continues to inspire us: "Right action requires only that we respond faithfully to our own inner truth and to the truth around us. . . . If an action is rightly taken, taken with integrity, its outcomes will achieve whatever is possible—which is the best that anyone can do" (1990, p. 115).

Robert D. Reason
Ellen M. Broido
Tracy L. Davis
Nancy J. Evans
Editors

References

Evans, N. J., and Reason, R. D. "Guiding Principles: A Review and Analysis of Student Affairs Philosophical Statements." *Journal of College Student Development*, 2001, *42*, 359–377.

Fish, S. "Why We Built the Ivory Tower." *New York Times*, May 21, 2004.

Horowitz, D. "In Defense of Intellectual Diversity." Feb. 10, 2004. [http://studentsfor academicfreedom.org/archive/February%202004/DHChroniclearticle021004.htm].

Palmer, P. *The Active Life: Wisdom for Work, Creativity, and Caring.* New York: Harper-Collins, 1990.

Wolf-Wendel, L. E., and others. *Reflecting Back, Looking Forward: Civil Rights and Student Affairs.* Washington, D.C.: National Association of Student Personnel Administrators, 2004.

ROBERT D. REASON *is assistant professor of education and professor-in-charge of the college student affairs program at Penn State University. He is also a research associate in Penn State's Center for the Study of Higher Education.*

ELLEN M. BROIDO *is assistant professor of higher education and student affairs at Bowling Green State University in Ohio.*

TRACY L. DAVIS *is associate professor of college student personnel and program coordinator in the educational and interdisciplinary studies department at Western Illinois University.*

NANCY J. EVANS *is professor and co-coordinator of the higher education program in the department of educational leadership and policy studies at Iowa State University.*

1

The authors explore the relationships between social justice attitudes and actions, the social construction of identity, and cognitive development.

Antecedents, Precursors, and Concurrent Concepts in the Development of Social Justice Attitudes and Actions

Robert D. Reason, Tracy L. Davis

The college-going population is growing increasingly diverse (National Center for Education Statistics, 2003). This increasing diversity requires students to understand cultural differences in order to interact across social groups on college campuses successfully. Unfortunately, increasing segregation in American high schools means that substantial intergroup interactions often occur for the first time at colleges and universities (Orfield, Bachmeier, James, and Eitle, 1997). Positive intergroup relations are critical to achieving social justice "because studies show that judgments about what is 'just', 'fair', or 'deserved' are central social judgments that lie at the heart of people's feelings, attitudes, and behaviors in their interactions with others" (Tyler and Smith, 1998, p. 595).

Research continues to highlight the deleterious effects of negative intergroup interactions on the learning environments and learning outcomes for all students (Hurtado and others, 2002; Gurin, Dey, Hurtado, and Gurin, 2002). Research also shows that college students in nonmajority social groups have differential access to resources before college, which often hinders their educational attainment during college (Carnevale and Fry, 2002). To maximize student learning both in and out of the classroom, we must improve intergroup relations on campus and create an environment that nurtures all students equitably.

New Directions for Student Services, no. 110, Summer 2005 © Wiley Periodicals, Inc.

The development of social justice allies focuses on the role of members of the dominant groups in creating such a learning environment for all students. In this chapter, we introduce what we mean by social justice allies, attitudes, and actions and explore a series of related concepts. Starting with a common definition of social justice, a term that currently receives a good deal of attention in both popular and academic literature, we begin to examine how best to educate dominant group members to achieve social justice goals and improve learning. Furthermore, we explore the interrelated concepts of socially constructed identities, multiple identities, cognitive development, and resistance to social justice education.

Common Definitions

The increasingly diverse student population in higher education has given rise to an increased focus on social justice by the popular media, as well as among researchers and higher education administrators. A simple keyword search for *social justice* in the *Boston Globe*, for example, revealed over two hundred hits in a one-year period. A similar search of the *Chronicle of Higher Education* found fifty-four articles about social justice issues in the past three years, while a search of the Educational Resources Information Center resulted in seventy-eight identified articles about social justice in higher education between 2001 and 2003.

As with any other concept that receives such widespread attention, differences in understanding and definition emerge, often clouding the important discussion and hindering communication. A first step in encouraging the development of social justice allies therefore is arriving at a common understanding of what we mean by social justice.

Distributive and Procedural Justice. Social justice literature focuses on two types of justice: distributive and procedural (Wendorf, Alexander, and Firestone, 2002). Distributive justice refers to the distribution of limited goods and resources based on the principles of equity, need, or equality (Tyler and Smith, 1998). Those seeking distributive social justice are essentially concerned with the equitable distribution of benefits among the members of various social groups. Financial aid and admission to college, for example, are two limited resources that often enter the discussion of distributive justice in higher education (Cabrera and LaNasa, 2000; Heller, 2002). The manner in which these resources are distributed is a matter of social justice that concerns many educators.

Procedural justice focuses on influence during the decision-making process (Tyler and Smith, 1998). How much input one group has in the decision-making process relative to other groups is a matter of procedural justice. Participants likely will judge procedures fair if the decision-making process is deemed neutral, trustworthy, and respectful of others in the process (Tyler, 1994). Whereas the distribution of financial aid and admission to college is a distributional justice concern, the process by which decisions are made about the distribution of these resources is a procedural justice issue. One need only recall the University of Michigan affirmative action cases to recognize that procedural justice in college admissions is of national concern. Due process procedures in judicial matters on campus provide a more local example of a procedural justice issue.

Social Justice Ally Attitudes and Actions Defined. We conceptualize social justice in terms that combine both distributive and procedural justice toward a goal of full and equal participation for all groups, where resources are equitably distributed and everyone is physically and psychologically safe (Bell, 1997; Broido, 2000). Social justice *attitudes* are therefore beliefs about and judgments regarding the current status of achieving this goal. Social justice *actions* are behaviors taken on behalf of this goal. Social justice *allies*, the focus of this book, are "members of dominant social groups (e.g., men, Whites, heterosexuals) who are working to end the system of oppression that gives them greater privilege and power based upon their social group membership" (Broido, 2000, p. 3).

The development of social justice allies requires recognition of previously unexamined privilege, power, and prejudice (Washington and Evans, 1991). People from privileged groups rarely are called on to examine their dominant characteristic and the benefits that accompany it (Goodman, 2001). Caucasians, for example, rarely are forced to examine whiteness and the unearned privileges that accompany it in our society (McIntosh, 1989). Without recognition and examination of the benefits of dominant group membership, we are less likely to recognize the damages caused to those outside the dominant group (Goodman, 2001).

Although similar in many respects, the development of social justice allies is more than "prejudice prevention." Both concepts assume a proactive stance and maintain a goal of positive intergroup interactions, but prejudice prevention literature stresses "preventing the potential escalation and expressions of . . . prejudice" (Ponterotto and Pedersen, 1993, p. 9). The focus is on preventing negative action, whereas the emphasis of social justice ally development is on encouraging positive actions.

Ultimately the development of social justice allies must result in action that upsets the status quo—the dominant ideology and culture that maintains social inequality (Bergerson, 2003; Goodman, 2001). The status quo can be maintained consciously through active reinforcement as well as unconsciously through a lack of action. Failure to take action that upsets the status quo therefore maintains the dominant ideology. Thus, the development of social justice allies must focus on the translation of attitudes into action if anything is to change.

Diversity, Multiculturalism, and Social Justice. The concept of social justice, as just defined, is related to yet distinct from the concepts of diversity and multiculturalism. Talbot (1996) defined *diversity* as "a structure that includes the tangible presence of individuals representing a variety of different attributes and characteristics" and *multiculturalism* as "a state of being in which an individual feels comfortable and communicates effectively" across social groups (p. 381).

Although other more comprehensive definitions exist (Levin, 2003; Milem, 2003), *diversity* is often used to refer to the number or proportion of individuals with a specific characteristic in an environment. Gurin (1999) referred to this interpretation as "structural diversity." The proportions of women or Latinos on a college campus are measures of structural diversity. Multiculturalism, however, is a measure of an individual's ability to remove barriers to effective interactions. Whereas diversity is a quantifiable characteristic of an environment, multiculturalism is better conceptualized as a journey that is ongoing and developmental (Talbot, 1996).

Diversity, multiculturalism, and social justice are related to each other and to the educational outcomes achieved by college students. As Milem (2003) clearly stated, "Supporting diversity in colleges and universities is not only a matter of social justice but also a matter of promoting educational excellence" (p. 126). The research that Milem reviewed clearly indicated that structural diversity is a necessary foundation on which multicultural skills and social justice ally attitudes are developed. It is within diverse environments that multicultural skills are tested and refined. It is within diverse environments that social justice ally attitudes are most directly tested and turned into actions.

Related Processes

In order to better understand the process of social justice ally development, one must understand several related processes. In this section, we discuss the social construction of identity, the concept of multiple identities and subjectivities, and the cognitive development process as they relate to social justice ally development. We end with a discussion of resistance to social justice ally development.

The Social Construction of Identity. In the United States, we are socialized to believe in the sanctity of individual rights and the values of individualism (Pedersen, 1988; Triandis, 1994). One of the myths perpetuated by this ideology is that individual identity represents the autonomous, independent construction of self. In sharp contrast to this myth is the wealth of evidence that suggests our identities are critically influenced by traditions, history, context, and other cultural narratives (D'Augelli, 1994; Vygotsky, 1978; Young, 1990). Josselson (1996) argued, for example, that identity is "not just a private, individual matter [but] a complex negotiation between the person and society" (p. 31). The construction of identity therefore occurs as individuals negotiate cultural scripts.

Understanding identity as socially constructed interrupts the hegemonic assumption that people get what they deserve. Hegemony is essentially "the maintenance of domination not by the sheer exercise of force but primarily through consensual social practices, social forms, and social structures" (McLaren, 1998, p. 182). Focusing only on intra-individual developmental processes and ignoring the impact of one's cultural milieu is consistent with an assumption in Western civilization of rugged individualism. For social justice ally development to be successful, however, unconscious complicity with hegemonic individualism needs to be interrupted to allow for the possibility that people are either privileged or oppressed on the basis of social group status. For example, an adolescent African American female in the United States today is less likely to envision herself as president of this country than is a young Caucasian male. The former is a *target* for oppression and the latter an *agent* of privilege.

Targets are members of social identity groups who are disenfranchised and "kept in their place by the agents' ideology which supports oppression by denying its existence, and blames the condition of the oppressed on themselves and their own failings" (Adams, Bell, and Griffin, 1997, p. 20). Agents are "members of dominant social groups privileged by birth or acquisition, who knowingly or unknowingly exploit and reap unfair advantage over members of target groups" (p. 20). We develop these concepts of oppression and privilege, as well as agent and target identities, further in Chapter Two.

The implication of the social construction of identity for social justice ally development is therefore twofold. First, allies need to consider their privilege related to hegemonic individualism and other invisible cultural rules. Supporting this idea, Sleeter and Grant (1994) argued that social justice education should encourage students to reflect on their oppressed or privileged standing in order to judiciously understand the world around them. Similarly, in a study of students' understanding of social justice concepts, Chizhik and Chizhik (2002) found that "educators of social justice need to spend quality time dissecting the construct of privilege" (p. 806). Second, the social construction of identity creates critical learning space by emphasizing the role that the social environment has on learning. Students are equipped with the understanding that their prior knowledge has been shaped by historical and cultural contexts. This important awareness opens the door for creating the kind of shared understanding and co-construction of knowledge necessary for successful intergroup interaction.

Multiple Identities and Subjectivities. Developing social justice allies requires an understanding of the dynamics related to the social identity development of agents. Understanding these dynamics is complicated by the fact that there are multiple dimensions of identity. A model designed by Jones and McEwen (2000) illustrates this complexity. In their model, sexual orientation, race, culture, class, religion, and gender are identity dimensions that circulate around one's core identity. The salience of a particular dimension to one's core identity depends on changing contexts and is mediated by whether the dimension is experienced as a privilege or a difference. Thus, not only do people perceive identity dimensions both as externally defined and internally considered (that is, socially constructed), they may face one aspect of their identity as a target and others as an agent. For example, a white gay man from an upper socioeconomic class poses challenges to applying theories of oppression and social justice because he simultaneously holds membership in dominant and target groups that may (or may not) be visible to others.

In terms of social justice ally development, one possibility for promoting empathy and subsequent development may be to explore dimensions of identity where an individual has oppressed group experiences. O'Brien (2001) refers to this strategy as "overlapping approximations" (p. 27), in which an ally draws an analogy between a personal oppression and the oppression of others. Croteau, Talbot, Lance, and Evans (2002), however, found that while individuals could identify multiple social groups to which they belonged, they had difficulty understanding the interplay among their multiple social identities. They further found that the "weight, recognition, or value" (p. 246) individuals place on their privileged (or targeted) social identities affects the "weight, recognition, or value" they place on their targeted (or privileged) identities.

The concept of multiple identities also focuses attention on the complex social interaction between individuals. Consider, for example, a classroom discussion about oppression between a Latino Christian heterosexual female and a white Jewish gay male. The quality of this discussion will be mediated by the multiple dimensions of identity and the salience of each dimension for each person. This classroom example is further complicated by the fact that there is power associated with the student-teacher relationship. According to Cummins (2003), "Interactions between teachers and students are never neutral and educators have choices in the way they define their roles in relation to marginalized students and communities and in the kinds of interactions they orchestrate in their classrooms. These interactions construct an interpersonal space within which knowledge is generated and identities are negotiated" (p. 43). Analogous power differences exist in the relationships student affairs professionals forge with the students they teach. Clearly, multiple identities and subjectivities and related power dimensions need to be understood to successfully promote social justice ally development.

Cognitive Development. Theories of cognitive development (Baxter Magolda, 1992; Belenky, Clinchy, Goldberger, and Tarule, 1986; King and Kitchener, 1994; Perry, 1970) portray the shifts in worldviews from "concrete to abstract, simple to complex, external authority to internal agency, and clear-cut certitudes to comfort with doubt, uncertainty, and independent inquiry" (Adams, Bell, and Griffin, 1997, p. 41). Individuals who are in the first stages, perspectives, or ways of knowing in each of these theories (Perry's dualism or Baxter Magolda's absolute knowing, for example) insist on clear answers, look to teachers as authorities, and are intolerant of the ambiguity associated with the complexities of intercultural understanding. According to Adams, Bell, and Griffin (1997), these cognitive styles "are indicators of conceptual limits upon students' readiness to listen, respond to, and learn from each other's divergent experiences and viewpoints" (p. 41).

As students move out of a dualistic or received knowledge view of the world, they become more comfortable with multiple perspectives and the subjectivity of authority and knowing. With this important transition comes a new ability to examine different worldviews, understand one's own subjective biases, and more fully understand complex concepts like privilege, oppression, and intersubjectivity associated with social justice ally development. The value of cognitive growth for development of social justice allies is reinforced by Broido (2000), whose research suggested that "the ability to reason more complexly might allow one to be more aware of the dissonance between the democratic and egalitarian values of our culture and the realities of oppression" (p. 4). It makes sense that it is necessary for individuals to develop more complex reasoning skills in order to suspend hegemonic messages and accept the lack of absolutes in social justice problem solving.

Cognitive development must also be considered as educators choose strategies that advance social justice attitude development. The skills necessary to explore issues of social justice are quite cognitively complex (King and Shuford, 1996). Rios, Trent, and Castañeda (2003), for example, advocated the use of perspective taking and critical self-reflection to further students' understanding of social justice issues and personal privilege. Perspective taking and self-reflection are skills that college students may not acquire, however, until they have developed their cognitive complexity past dualism. Baxter Magolda (1992) placed the ability to assume another's perspective clearly in the Independent Knower stage, the third of her four stages. This strategy may be ineffective with many younger college students. As with all other teaching, then, social justice educators must join "students 'where they are'. . . . [and] encourage them to consider more complex ways of thinking" (p. 224).

Emotional Landscape and Resistance to Social Justice Education. The cognitive dissonance created by shifting perspectives on knowing can be threatening. According to Boler and Zembylas (2003), "To engage in critical inquiry often means asking students to radically reevaluate their worldviews. This process can incur feelings of anger, grief, disappointment and resistance" (p. 111). Thus, social justice education requires both cognitive and emotional effort.

The level of cognitive complexity a student brings to social justice education is related to the level of resistance the student may exhibit. For example, students who have a dualistic worldview may tend to "dichotomize complex questions, reduce multiple perspectives to simple either/or choices, or not see relations between complex personal examples and broader theoretical principles" (Adams, Jones, and Tatum, 1997, p. 321), all of which result in greater cognitive dissonance, emotional distress, and resistance to social justice education. Again, choosing strategies appropriate to the worldview of our students reduces resistance.

In addition to the cognitive attributes that provide a barrier to social justice ally development, Boler and Zembylas (2003) described three emotional stances that reflect resistance caused by difference education. These three emotional stances are responses to three models of difference that are consistent with dominant cultural myths of meritocracy and equal opportunity. The first model is called the *celebration* or *tolerance model.* From this perspective, difference is characterized by the idea that everyone is different and we should tolerate and respect all differences. This benign multicultural perspective, however fails to account for power differences and systematic discrimination (Boler and Zembylas, 2003).

A second model is termed *denial* or *sameness.* Those espousing this perspective are likely to be frustrated at what they feel is too much attention to difference and claim that "we are all essentially the same." Once again, this model ignores issues of power and the privilege to determine which differences are important. The third perspective is the *natural response* or *biological model.* From this viewpoint, some differences are seen as innate, and fear is seen as a natural human response to difference. Dismissing differences as essentially immutable excuses one from attending to the complex intersections between individual and sociopolitical influences.

Failure to understand the social construction of identity, social identity development theory, and multiple dimensions of identity, along with the cognitive and affective characteristics, likely results in resistance to social justice education and ally development. This understanding underscores the interconnectedness of the various concepts related to social justice ally development discussed in this chapter.

Successful pedagogical strategies aimed at encouraging social justice allies will honor these causes of resistance. Goodman (2001) suggested building supportive learning environments through proactive and confirming strategies that mirror strategies suggested by Baxter Magolda (1992): validating the student as knower, situating learning in the students' own experiences, and jointly constructing understanding. Knowing students and planning educational interventions that anticipate cognitive and affective resistance, acknowledging and exploring the root causes of resistance, and disclosing personal experiences are strategies that may reduce resistance.

Conclusion

The development of social justice allies requires more than one more diversity or sensitivity workshop. We and the other chapter authors advocate throughout the rest of this volume a planned, thoughtful approach to developing social justice allies. Student affairs professionals who are responsible for planning educational experiences for dominant group members must consider what we already know about students, especially what cognitive development theories tell us, meet our students where they are, and nurture them through what is likely to be a cognitive and emotionally painful journey. We believe the payoff of the journey, for our students and our-selves, is worth the trip. As our society continues to diversify, we must not only equip students with the skills for positive cross-cultural interactions, but also enlist their help in eliminating barriers to true social justice.

References

Adams, M., Bell, L. A., and Griffin, P. *Teaching for Diversity and Social Justice: A Sourcebook.* New York: Routledge, 1997.

Adams, M., Jones, J., and Tatum, B. D. "Knowing Our Students." In M. Adams, L. A. Bell, and P. Griffin (eds.), *Teaching for Diversity and Social Justice: A Sourcebook.* New York: Routledge, 1997.

Baxter Magolda, M. B. *Knowing and Reasoning in College: Gender-Related Patterns in Students' Intellectual Development.* San Francisco: Jossey-Bass, 1992.

Belenky, M. E., Clinchy, M. B., Goldberger, N. R., and Tarule, J. M. *Women's Ways of Knowing: The Development of Self, Voice, and Mind.* New York: Basic Books, 1986.

Bell, L. A. "Theoretical Foundations for Social Justice Education." In M. Adams, L. A. Bell, and P. Griffin (eds.), *Teaching for Diversity and Social Justice—A Sourcebook.* New York: Routledge, 1997.

Bergerson, A. A. "Critical Race Theory and White Racism: Is There Room for White Scholars in Righting Racism in Education?" *Qualitative Studies in Education,* 2003, 16(1), 51–63.

Boler, M., and Zembylas, M. "Discomforting Truths: The Emotional Terrain of Understanding Difference." In P. P. Trifonas (ed.), *Pedagogies of Difference: Rethinking Education for Social Change.* New York: RoutledgeFalmer, 2003.

Broido, E. M. "The Development of Social Justice Allies During College: A Phenomenological Investigation." *Journal of College Student Development,* 2000, 41, 3–18.

Cabrera, A. F., and LaNasa, S. M. "Understanding the College-Choice Process." In A. F. Cabrera and S. M. LaNasa (eds.), *Understanding the College Choice of Disadvantaged Students.* New Directions in Institutional Research, no. 107. San Francisco: Jossey-Bass, 2000.

Carnevale, A. P., and Fry, R. A. "The Demographic Window of Opportunity: College Access and Diversity in the New Century." In D. E. Heller (ed.), *Condition of Access: Higher Education for Lower Income Students.* Westport, Conn.: Praeger, 2002.

Chizhik, E. W., and Chizhik, A. W. "What Do Privilege and Oppression Really Mean?" *Journal of College Student Development,* 2002, 43, 792–808.

Croteau, J. M., Talbot, D. M., Lance, T. S., and Evans, N. J. "A Qualitative Study of the Interplay Between Privilege and Oppression." *Journal of Multicultural Counseling and Development,* 2002, 30, 239–258.

Cummins, J. "Challenging the Construction of Difference as Deficit: Where Are Identity, Intellect, Imagination, and Power in the New Regime of Truth?" In P. P. Trifonas (ed.), *Pedagogies of Difference: Rethinking Education for Social Change.* New York: RoutledgeFalmer, 2003.

D'Augelli, A. R. "Identity Development and Sexual Orientation: Toward a Model of Lesbian, Gay, and Bisexual Development." In E. J. Trickett, R. J. Watts, and D. Birman (eds.), *Human Diversity: Perspectives on People in Context.* San Francisco: Jossey-Bass, 1994.

Goodman, D. J. *Promoting Diversity and Social Justice: Educating People from Privileged Groups.* Thousand Oaks, Calif.: Sage, 2001.

Gurin, P. "Expert Report: 'Gratz et al. v. Bollinger, et al.' No. 97–75321 (E.D. Mich); 'Grutter, et al. v. Bollinger, et al.' No. 97–75928 (E.D. Mich.)." *Equity and Excellence in Education,* 1999, 32, 36–62.

Gurin, P., Dey, E. L., Hurtado, S., and Gurin, G. "Diversity and Higher Education: Theory and Impact on Educational Outcomes." *Harvard Educational Review*, 2002, *72*, 330–365.

Heller, D. E. (ed.). *Conditions of Access: Higher Education for Lower Income Students.* Westport, Conn.: American Council on Education/Praeger, 2002.

Hurtado, S., and others. "Intergroup Relations: Views from Different Racial/Ethnic Groups." Paper presented at the Association for Institutional Research Forum, Toronto, June 2002.

Jones, S. R., and McEwen, M. K. "A Conceptual Model of Multiple Dimensions of Identity." *Journal of College Student Development*, 2000, *41*(4), 405–414.

Josselson, R. *Revising Herself: The Story of Women's Identity from College to Midlife.* New York: Oxford University Press, 1996.

King, P. M., and Kitchener, K. S. *Developing Reflective Judgment: Understanding and Promoting Intellectual Growth and Critical Thinking in Adolescents and Adults.* San Francisco: Jossey-Bass, 1994.

King, P. M., and Shuford, B. C. "A Multicultural View Is a More Cognitively Complex View: Cognitive Development and Multicultural Education." *American Behavioral Scientist*, 1996, *40*, 153–164.

Levin, S. "Social and Psychological Evidence on Race and Racism." In M. J. Chang, D. Witt, J. Jones, and K. Hakuta (eds.), *Compelling Interest: Examining the Evidence on Racial Dynamics in Colleges and Universities.* Stanford, Calif.: Stanford University Press, 2003.

McIntosh, P. "White Privilege: Unpacking the Invisible Knapsack." *Peace and Freedom,* July–Aug. 1989, pp. 10–12.

McLaren, P. *Life in Schools: An Introduction to Critical Pedagogy in the Foundations of Education.* White Plains, N.Y.: Longman, 1998.

Milem, J. F. "The Educational Benefits of Diversity: Evidence from Multiple Sectors." In M. J. Chang, D. Witt, J. Jones, and K. Hakuta (eds.), *Compelling Interest: Examining the Evidence on Racial Dynamics in Colleges and Universities.* Stanford, Calif.: Stanford University Press, 2003.

National Center for Education Statistics. "Projection of Education Statistics to 2013." 2003. [http://nces.ed.gov/programs/projections].

O'Brien, E. *Whites Confront Racism: Antiracists and Their Paths to Action.* Lanham, Md.: Rowman and Littlefield, 2001.

Orfield, G., Bachmeier, M. D., James, D. R., and Eitle, T. "Deepening Segregation in American Public Schools: A Special Report from the Harvard Project on School Desegregation." *Equity and Excellence in Education*, 1997, *30*(2), 5–24.

Pedersen, P. *A Handbook for Developing Multicultural Awareness.* Alexandria, Va.: American Association for Counseling and Development, 1988.

Perry, W. G. *Forms of Intellectual and Ethical Development in the College Years.* New York: Holt, 1970.

Ponterotto, J. G., and Pedersen, P. B. *Prejudice Prevention: A Guide for Counselors and Educators.* Thousand Oaks, Calif.: Sage, 1993.

Rios, F., Trent, A., and Castañeda, L. V. "Social Perspective Taking: Advancing Empathy and Advocating Justice." *Equity and Excellence in Education*, 2003, *36*(1), 5–14.

Sleeter, C., and Grant, C. *Making Choices for Multicultural Education: Five Approaches to Race, Class, and Gender.* New York: Merrill, 1994.

Talbot, D. M. "Multiculturalism." In S. R. Komives and D. B. Woodard Jr. (eds.), *Student Services: A Handbook for the Profession.* (3rd ed.) San Francisco: Jossey-Bass, 1996.

Triandis, H. C. *Culture and Social Behavior.* New York: McGraw-Hill, 1994.

Tyler, T. R. "Psychological Models of the Justice Motive: Antecedents of Distributive and Procedural Justice." *Journal of Personality and Social Psychology*, 1994, *67*, 850–863.

Tyler, T. R., and Smith, H. J. "Social Justice and Social Movements." In D. T. Gilbert, S. T. Fiske, and G. Lindzey (eds.), *The Handbook of Social Psychology.* (4th ed.) New York: McGraw-Hill, 1998.

Vygotsky, L. *Mind in Society.* Cambridge, Mass.: Harvard University Press, 1978.

Washington, J., and Evans, N. J. "Becoming an Ally." In N. J. Evans and V. A. Wall (eds.), *Beyond Tolerance: Gays, Lesbians, and Bisexuals on Campus.* Washington, D.C.: American College Personnel Association, 1991.

Wendorf, C. A., Alexander, S., and Firestone, I. J. "Social Justice and Moral Reasoning: An Empirical Integration of Two Paradigms in Psychological Research." *Social Justice Research,* 2002, *15,* 19–39.

Young, I. M. *Justice and the Politics of Difference.* Princeton, N.J.: Princeton University Press, 1990.

ROBERT D. REASON is assistant professor of education and professor-in-charge of the college student affairs program at Penn State University. He is also a research associate in Penn State's Center for the Study of Higher Education.

TRACY L. DAVIS is associate professor of college student personnel and program coordinator in the educational and interdisciplinary studies department at Western Illinois University.

2

This chapter reviews the current theoretical understanding of the development of social justice attitudes and related concepts.

The Development of Social Justice Attitudes and Actions: An Overview of Current Understandings

Ellen M. Broido, Robert D. Reason

As Allan Johnson (2000) noted, "The simple truth is that [social injustice] can't be solved unless people who are heterosexual or male or Anglo or White or economically comfortable feel obligated to make the problem of privilege *their* problem and to do something about it" (p. 10). This chapter explores ways in which college students have come to do something about it, looking first at general theories of student learning and change during college, models of ally development based on noncollege populations, and Broido's model of college student ally development. The chapter closes with a discussion of ways in which the college environment can be shaped to foster the development of allies.

Student Learning During College

Students enter college with previous experiences, attitudes, and behaviors that influence their experiences and outcomes. Focusing only on what happens to students at college ignores the importance of the characteristics developed prior to attendance. This intuitive understanding was conceptualized in Astin's input-environment-output (I-E-O) model (1993), which underlies our understanding of change during college. Although other researchers (Terenzini, Springer, Pascarella, and Nora, 1995) have expanded and made more specific Astin's original model, it remains the foundational framework for understanding change in college students.

NEW DIRECTIONS FOR STUDENT SERVICES, no. 110, Summer 2005 © Wiley Periodicals, Inc.

Astin's Input-Experience-Output Model. Writing for researchers, Astin (1993) indicated that an assessment of student learning was incomplete if it did not include data on "student inputs, student outcomes, and the educational environment to which they are exposed" (p. 18). A thorough understanding of students' learning about social justice and development as allies during college also must incorporate data from these three areas. We are interested in how an outcome (social justice attitudes and actions) is influenced by the environment (college experiences) after considering the relevant inputs (precollege characteristics).

Inputs are personal characteristics and qualities students bring to college (Astin, 1993). Environmental variables include factors related to a student's experiences at college; often these are the variables over which we have the most control. Finally, the outcome is the skill, talent, or characteristic we are attempting to develop in students.

To fully understand which environmental variables most influence the development of social justice allies, we need to incorporate (or control for) relevant input variables, including personal characteristics such as race, ethnicity, gender, and socioeconomic status. The social justice attitudes students bring with them to college, exposure to diverse others in high school, and precollege involvement in social justice actions are other input variables particularly related to our outcome variable.

Other Models of Student Learning. Astin's I-E-O model (1993) is most useful in identifying environmental variables (Terenzini and Upcraft, 1996). Terenzini, Springer, Pascarella, and Nora (1995) expanded Astin's model to clarify the environmental component, which helps further identify those experiences over which institutions may have some control. Researchers identified four sources of influence on college students' change. The first is precollege characteristics, which are comparable to Astin's conceptualization of input variables. The following three sources are expanded breakdowns of Astin's definition of *environment:* (1) the institutional context, (2) academic experiences, and (3) cocurricular experiences (Flowers and Pascarella, 1999; Terenzini, Springer, Pascarella, and Nora, 1995). Student change and learning is a function of the complex interactions among these four sources of influence.

According to Terenzini, Springer, Pascarella, and Nora (1995), the "interplay between and among [the other variables that influence student change] takes place within a particular institutional context (for example, organizational characteristics, structures, and policies)" (p. 26). It also includes students' perceptions of the institutional climate.

Academic experiences include variables related to courses and course patterns, as well as in-class experiences (Terenzini, Springer, Pascarella, and Nora, 1995). Students' academic majors, course distribution across disciplines, number of diversity and social justice courses taken, and credit hours taken would constitute courses and course pattern data. In-class experience encompasses variables related to in-class interactions between students and teachers, or teacher effectiveness. The inclusion of active teaching methods or experiential learning activities would also fall under this category.

Students' out-of-class experiences constitute the third component of environmental variables. Research related to social justice education indicates that the amount and quality of out-of-class experiences with diverse others are influential in the development of social justice allies (Milem, 2003). Other possible variables to consider are students' participation in diversity workshops and trainings and student groups related to social justice issues.

Models of Ally Development

Many have conceptualized the development of social justice attitudes in ways that reflect the I-E-O approach (Bishop, 2002; Chojnacki and Gelberg, 1995; Fabiano and others, 2003; Hardiman and Jackson, 1992, 1997). Bishop and Hardiman and Jackson offer conceptualizations that are both broadly applicable and possess the characteristics of a developmental understanding.

Bishop: Becoming an Ally. Bishop (2002) provided a six-step framework for understanding the development of social justice allies that combines both cognitive and behavioral components. Although writing specifically about interracial social justice allies, Bishop contextualized power and privilege broadly, which makes her framework a useful tool to understand all social justice ally development.

Bishop suggested that the development of social justice allies begins with understanding oppression. This understanding should include how oppression began, how it is maintained, and how it stamps its pattern on the individuals and institutions that continually recreate it. According to Bishop, allies must recognize oppression as part of societal structures, which makes it both self-sustaining and difficult to eradicate.

"All oppressions are interdependent, they all come from the same worldview, and none can be solved in isolation" (Bishop, 2002, p. 20). The second step in her model therefore is to recognize and understand the interactions among different oppressions. Bishop suggested that separation between groups, the tendency to place oppressions in a hierarchy, and the need for social groups to compete for resources may be alleviated when the similarities among oppressions are recognized and confronted collectively. Social justice allies thus become more effective when they are able to articulate the similarities and interactions between oppressions.

Pain accompanies an increased understanding of one's role in the cycle of oppression (Bishop, 2002). Bishop suggested that healing this pain (step three) is essential to breaking the cycle of oppression and growing as a social justice ally. Before you can become an ally of others, however, you must become "a worker in your own liberation" (p. 100). The fourth step in Bishop's model therefore is to recognize areas where oppression touches each of us and to take action toward change.

Step five, becoming an ally, requires that each of us examine our previous roles as oppressors and learn a new skill set as allies (Bishop, 2002). Bishop recognized a defined role for dominant group members in working for the liberation of target group members and provided suggestions to be effective allies. Allies must focus on listening to and supporting others rather than leading (or co-opting) the movement of the target group. The action of allies, according to Bishop, must be within the dominant group to which they belong; allies must educate their dominant group peers about oppressive behaviors and systems.

Finally, Bishop (2002) recognized that being an active social justice ally is difficult. In step six in her model, she therefore discussed the importance of maintaining hope and idealism while working for social change. Recognizing a social movement as a long-term journey and holding to the sincere belief that what is learned (racism, sexism, homophobia) can be unlearned is requisite for sustaining a social justice ally identity.

Hardiman and Jackson: Social Identity Development Theory. Social identity, according to Hardiman and Jackson (1992, 1997), is a function of the degree to which individuals accept external messages about their social group. They suggested that members of dominant and target groups consciously and intentionally accept (or reject) the oppressive messages about superiority of some social groups. Ultimately individuals move toward a redefinition and internalization of a social identity that is independent of hierarchical and oppressive relationships toward other groups. Since the focus of this volume is on allies, who by definition are dominant group members, only dominant group processes are discussed here.

As with many other identity theories based on a constructivist paradigm (for example, Cross, 1991, and Helms, 1990), Hardiman and Jackson's theory assumes that individuals begin with little or no understanding of their own identities. Movement out of this naive stage normally occurs when external messages about social acceptability and hierarchy are incorporated into the understanding of one's social group. Young boys, for example, incorporate the implicit and explicit messages they receive about girls and boys. This Acceptance stage (Hardiman and Jackson, 1992, 1997) is characterized by the belief that agents (boys) are superior and targets (girls) are inferior. Most boys learn early that they should construct a social identity that has few, if any, characteristics that might be considered "girlish" or feminine.

"As a result of experiences and information that challenges the accepted ideology and self-definition, agents entering Resistance reject earlier social positions and begin formulating a new world view" (Hardiman and Jackson, 1997, p. 26). It is in this stage that members of the dominant groups begin to recognize and own the privileges associated with their group membership. Furthermore, dominant group members begin to critically examine and ultimately reject the roles they have played in the oppression of target group members.

In the Redefinition and Internalization stages, members of the dominant group develop and incorporate a positive social identity, "independent of an oppressive system based on hierarchical superiority" (Hardiman and Jackson, 1997, p. 27). During the Internalization stage, new social justice values are incorporated into action (Hardiman and Jackson, 1992, 1997).

Broido's Model of College Student Ally Development

Although useful to our overall understanding social justice ally development, most treatments tend to be atheoretical or not empirically derived. At this time, only one study (Broido, 1997, 2000) has looked specifically at how college experiences affect the development of social justice allies. In this phenomenological study, six white, heterosexual students (three women and three men) discussed their development as allies during college, how they understood their own identities, and their experiences doing ally work. From their description of their experiences, the following patterns became clear.

Precollege Attitudes. Participants in this study entered college with generally open, accepting attitudes about people different from themselves. Although they often had little specific knowledge about people different from themselves, they were open to learning. All but one had grown up in communities that were predominantly white. They also lacked any theoretical frameworks for understanding the systemic and institutional nature of oppression, as well as little knowledge of the extent, impact, and dynamics of oppression on target group members or of the benefits and privileges accruing to dominant group members as a group. What they did have was a basic egalitarian belief in the espoused values of American culture that everyone should have equal opportunity, all people have value, and fairness was critical.

Acquiring Information. Learning new information about a variety of aspects of social justice was critical for participants in their development as allies. Much of the learning happened in traditional academic settings, particularly in courses in sociology, women's studies, and training classes for resident assistants. Participants also reported learning things critical to their development as allies from target group members directly, from their dominant group peers (from whom they learned how common, and extreme, oppressive views still were), from their interactions with residence life staff members, from international travel, and from independent reading. These interactions occurred both in and out of class settings, although rarely in activities formally recognized or organized by student affairs staff (they did not happen in educational programs about diversity or student organizations, for example).

Participants reported learning facts and statistics about oppression and its continued existence and about the experiences of target group members, their own privilege as dominant group members, connections among various forms of oppression, and the benefits of a more diverse and socially just society. Less traditional learnings included becoming aware of the existence and work of social justice allies, the nature and extent of their peers' prejudices and lack of knowledge, strategies for conducting social justice activism, and the importance of activism.

Meaning Making. The participants in this study used three mutually interacting strategies to make meaning of the various forms of information they had acquired: discussion, self-reflection, and perspective taking. These students did not just passively absorb information; they talked about it with others; reflected on their own experiences, thoughts, and feelings; and tried to see the world through others' eyes. Through these processes, they were able to more clearly articulate their own beliefs and values regarding social justice issues and develop a solid knowledge base.

Confidence: In Themselves, in Their Views, and in Their Knowledge Bases. Confidence played a surprisingly significant role in the development of social justice allies and appeared in various forms throughout the participants' stories. Two critical forms of confidence resulted from the learning described above: as participants more clearly knew what they believed regarding social justice issues, they developed greater confidence in their beliefs. And as their knowledge bases increased, they grew more confident in themselves as having the authority to speak to these issues.

General self-confidence—comfort with their own identities, strong senses of self-worth, and lack of need for external approval—was another critical factor in these students' development as social justice allies. This factor seemed to develop largely independent of the participants' work on social justice issues and came from a variety of sources, including taking on leadership roles, seniority, and clear knowledge of their own identities. Their comfort challenging others' views and the ability to withstand attacks on their identities were closely connected with this form of development. As one participant said, "I don't think you could do that [consider your own privilege] unless you still felt good about yourself, that you could take that kind of demotion."

Skill Development. Knowing what one believed, having information about social justice issues, and having self-confidence were all critical components of ally development for the participants in this study. One participant did directly discuss learning the skills necessary to do ally work; perhaps because his ally work was in many ways more conventionally activist and political than that of the other participants, it was important for him to learn behaviors that were distinct from those of his everyday life. This participant discussed learning to organize demonstrations, write letters to newspapers and elected officials, and work with the media. Another participant indicated that it would be easier for college students to become involved with social justice issues if the university were to put together an activist's handbook that would detail ways to create student organizations, university policies regarding protests and demonstrations, and other related topics.

The Importance of Chance and Recruitment. Knowledge, attitudes, and skills all were necessary precursors to ally behaviors, but at least for these participants, these were not sufficient for actual action as an ally. The only exception to this was one participant who had precollege experience doing social activism regarding issues around her target group memberships. For the other participants, ally behavior happened only when they were recruited into the work, they took on jobs or roles where such behaviors were expected of them, or through chance encounters. Largely, the participants did not initially seek out ally involvement on their own initiative.

Participants cited a number of examples of the role of chance in their initial development as allies. Classes that proved to be transformative were taken because they were offered at convenient times or seemed the least onerous of options for fulfilling a requirement. Chance introductions to others involved in social justice work led to invitations to attend rallies. Opportunities to get involved in social justice activities were offered earlier than opportunities for other equally interesting forms of involvement. Several participants discussed being recruited into their initial social justice actions: friends invited them to attend a protest, help circulate a petition, or staff a table gathering signatures to challenge racial graffiti. Others took on jobs where there was an expectation that they would educate others about social justice issues (for example, work as a resident assistant), even though their interest in the position was unrelated to any previous commitment to social justice issues.

Impact of College on Social Justice Ally Development

These models provide a framework for understanding how particular experiences fit together to foster the growth of allies. In this section, we review the literature that reports findings about specific college experiences that might foster this development. Little has been written about the impact of college experiences on social justice ally development specifically; however, much literature examines concepts related to social justice ally development. This section focuses on the literature that is most closely related to our definition of social justice ally development, notably the work originating from the Preparing Students for a Diverse Democracy project at the University of Michigan (http://www.umich.edu/~divdemo). Findings from this project are particularly appropriate for our purposes because they examined the relationships between college experiences and such outcomes as the importance students place on social action engagement (Hurtado, Engberg, and Punjuan, 2003), social awareness development (Greene and Kamimura, 2003), and the development of a pluralistic orientation (Engberg, Meader, and Hurtado, 2003). From this research and the research of others, we know that social justice ally development can be affected by formal and informal interactions, courses and workshops, and the messages institutions send to their students.

Interaction with Diverse Peers. Several discernable consistencies emerged in this literature, the most obvious of which is the importance of interaction with diverse peers. Universally, these authors found that interaction with a diverse friendship group resulted in increased growth in social justice–related outcomes. Related research studying openness to diversity (Whitt and others, 2001) and the development of tolerance (Taylor, 1998) confirms the importance of a network of diverse peers.

Several recent studies highlight the importance of the quality of diverse interactions (Milem, 2003). Chang (2001) concluded that diverse friendships that allowed serious discussions of social issues resulted in a decrease in racism for white students. Pike (2000), studying residence hall students, found that students with more intensity of information sharing through conversation with diverse others showed greater growth in openness to diversity. Finally, Hurtado and her colleagues (2002) reported that white students who studied with students from different racial groups developed greater pluralistic orientation.

Course Work and Workshops. Participation in courses or workshops related to issues of diversity also appears to influence outcomes related to social justice ally development, which may be a function of the quality of interaction that can occur in such settings. Palmer (2000), Springer and others (1996), and Whitt and others (2001) found a direct relationship between participation in educational sessions related to diversity and change in students' attitudes. Structured educational sessions may be particularly powerful for women (Smith, 1993) and students who might be initially resistant to diversity (Springer and others, 1996).

Courses and workshops that provide a safe environment to explore diversity issues and allow healthy conflict among individuals result in social justice outcomes (Hurtado, Engberg, and Ponjuan, 2003). Hurtado, Engberg, and Ponjuan suggest a strong experiential component to diversity and social justice courses to increase dialogue across groups. Facilitators should also attend to procedures for constructively resolving conflict and negotiating differences. Course work is not a panacea, however. In a study both interesting and disturbing, Henderson-King and Kaleta (2000) found that "in the absence of courses that focus on social diversity, undergraduate [white] students become less tolerant of others over a semester of undergraduate education" (p. 156). They interpreted their findings to mean that for most students, diversity course work, rather than creating more accepting attitudes about social diversity, only forestalls a decline in tolerance.

Institutional Characteristics. As Terenzini, Springer, Pascarella, and Nora (1995) highlighted, education occurs within an institutional context. Research suggests that the institutional context in which educational experiences occur has a direct effect on outcomes related to social justice. Whitt and others (2001), for example, found a relationship between students' perceptions of institutional support for diversity and students' openness to diversity and challenge. Institutions that convey a strong commitment to diversity therefore may support the development of social justice allies, although more research is needed to strengthen this claim. Rowley, Hurtado, and Ponjuan (2002) concluded, "To achieve a strong institutional commitment to diversity . . . a set of interlocking commitments to diversity must go beyond the rhetoric of mission statements to include articulation of diversity priorities, activities that evaluate and reward progress, core leadership support, and the development of a diverse student body" (p. 21).

Recommendations for Design of Campus Environments

The research reviewed here presents a number of recommendations for how ally development might be supported by college administrators and faculty. Consistent in the literature is the importance of contact with target group members, acquisition of knowledge about social justice issues, and self-reflection and reflection on learning. Also important are clarity of values regarding social justice issues, self-confidence, and recruitment. University personnel might facilitate students' engagement in these activities by asking students to talk with them about what they are learning, discuss their values, and examine how their behaviors align with those values. Students should be offered opportunities to interact with target group members in ways that facilitate sharing of experiences and mutual learning. Course work that deals with race and class, women's studies classes, and other social justice classes are critical to the development of allies.

Student affairs professionals, especially those at upper levels of the administration, have some level of power that students do not share. These professionals share a responsibility to influence change on their campuses (Evans and Reason, 2001), intervening not only at the individual student level but also at the institutional level. We offer the following suggestions for institution-level action:

• *Support the recruitment and retention of a diverse student body.* Many of the suggestions for encouraging social justice actions in dominant group students assume a substantial level of interaction across differences. Without a level of structural diversity on campus, gained through the active recruitment and retention of diverse students, high-quality interactions become difficult.

• *Study and improve campus climates.* The importance of students' perceptions of campus climate to learning and developmental outcomes is well documented. Campus climates also influence the level and quality of interactions among diverse students (Milem, 2003). Student affairs professionals thus should implement comprehensive assessments of the climates experienced on their campuses, identify areas for improvement based on those assessments, and work diligently to make those improvements.

• *Advocate for appropriate course work.* Empirical research highlights the importance of social justice courses in the development of social justice attitudes (Broido, 2000; Hurtado, Engberg, and Ponjuan, 2003; Reason, Roosa Millar, and Scales, 2004). If such course work is not currently available at their campuses, student affairs professionals should advocate for its development. Furthermore, nothing indicates institutional support on a college campus more than inclusion in the curriculum as a for-credit course. Developing social justice courses may thus carry the secondary benefit of signaling institutional support for social justice.

The material covered in this chapter addresses only developmental models and research that directly relates to college students. There exist multiple additional literature bases that speak to attitude change, motivations for ally work, and other aspects of social justice work. Perhaps the most assuring conclusion from the existing literature base is that the environments created on college campuses have the potential to influence students' development as allies. The following chapters explore specific programs and policies that foster the development of allies for specific oppressed groups.

References

Astin, A. W. *Assessment for Excellence: The Philosophy and Practice of Assessment and Evaluation in Higher Education.* New York: American Council on Education and Macmillan, 1993.

Bishop, A. *Becoming an Ally: Breaking the Cycle of Oppression in People.* (2nd ed.) Halifax, Nova Scotia: Fernwood, 2002.

Broido, E. M. "The Development of Social Justice Allies During College: A Phenomenological Investigation." *Dissertation Abstracts International,* 1997, *58*(12), 4577A.

Broido, E. M. "The Development of Social Justice Allies During College: A Phenomenological Investigation." *Journal of College Student Development,* 2000, *41,* 3–18.

Chang, M. "Is It More Than About Getting Along? The Broader Educational Relevance of Reducing Students' Racial Biases." *Journal of College Student Development,* 2001, *42,* 93–105.

Chojnacki, J. T., and Gelberg, S. "The Facilitation of a Gay/Lesbian/Bisexual Support Therapy Group by Heterosexual Counselors." *Journal of Counseling and Development,* 1995, *73,* 352–354.

Cross, W. E., Jr. *Shades of Black: Diversity in African American Identity.* Philadelphia: Temple University Press. 1991.

Engberg, M. E., Meader, E. W., and Hurtado, S. "Developing a Pluralistic Orientation: A Comparison of Ethnic Minority and White College Students." Paper presented at the Annual Meeting of the American Educational Research Association, Chicago, Apr. 2003.

Evans, N. J., and Reason, R. D. "Guiding Principles: A Review and Analysis of Student Affairs Philosophical Statements." *Journal of College Student Development,* 2001, *42,* 359–377.

Fabiano, P. M., and others. "Engaging Men as Social Justice Allies in Ending Violence Against Women: Evidence for a Social Norms Approach." *Journal of American College Health,* 2003, *52*(3), 105–112.

Flowers, L., and Pascarella, E. T. "Does College Racial Composition Influence the Openness to Diversity of African American Students?" *Journal of College Student Development*, 1999, *40*, 377–389.

Greene, S. R., and Kamimura, M. "Ties That Bind: Enhanced Social Awareness Development Through Interaction with Diverse Peers." Paper presented at the Annual Meeting of the Association for the Study of Higher Education, Portland, Ore., Nov. 2003.

Hardiman, R., and Jackson, B. W. "Racial Identity Development: Understanding Racial Dynamics in College Classrooms and on Campus." In M. Adams (ed.), *Promoting Diversity in College Classrooms: Innovative Responses for the Curriculum, Faculty, and Institution*. New Directions for Teaching and Learning, no. 52. San Francisco: Jossey-Bass, 1992.

Hardiman, R., and Jackson, B. W. "Conceptual Foundations for Social Justice Courses." In M. Adams, L. A. Bell, and P. Griffin (eds.), *Teaching for Diversity and Social Justice: A Sourcebook*. New York: Routledge, 1997.

Helms, J. E. "Toward a Model of White Racial Identity Development." In J. E. Helms (ed.), *Black and White Racial Identity: Theory, Research, and Practice*. Westport, Conn.: Greenwood Press, 1990.

Henderson-King, D., and Kaleta, A. "Learning About Social Diversity: The Undergraduate Experience and Intergroup Tolerance." *Journal of Higher Education*, 2000, *71*(special issue), 142–164. [http://links.jstor.org/sici?sici=0022–1546%28200003%2F04%2971%3A2%3C142%3ALASDTU%3E2.0.CO%3B2-M].

Hurtado, S., Engberg, M. E., and Ponjuan, L. "The Impact of the College Experience on Students' Learning for a Diverse Democracy." Paper presented at the annual meeting of the Association for the Study of Higher Education, Portland, Ore., Nov. 2003.

Hurtado, S., and others. "Intergroup Relations: Views from Different Racial/Ethnic Groups." Paper presented at the Association for Institutional Research Forum, Toronto, June 2002.

Johnson, A. *Privilege, Power, and Difference*. New York: McGraw-Hill, 2000.

Milem, J. F. "The Educational Benefits of Diversity: Evidence from Multiple Sectors." In M. J. Chang, D. Witt, J. Jones, and K. Hakuta (eds.), *Compelling Interest: Examining the Evidence on Racial Dynamics in Colleges and Universities*. Stanford, Calif.: Stanford University Press, 2003.

Palmer, B. "The Impact of Diversity Courses: Research from the Pennsylvania State University." *Diversity Digest*, Winter 2000, pp. 4–5.

Pike, G. R. "The Differential Effect of On- and Off-Campus Living Arrangements on Students' Openness to Diversity." *NASPA Journal*, 2000, *39*, 283–299.

Reason, R. D., Roosa Millar, E. A., and Scales, T. C. "Toward a Model of Interracial Social Justice Ally Development." Paper presented at the annual conference of the Association for the Study of Higher Education, Kansas City, Mo., Nov. 2004.

Rowley, L. L., Hurtado, S., and Ponjuan, L. "Organizational Rhetoric or Reality? The Disparities Between Avowed Commitment to Diversity and Formal Programs and Initiatives in Higher Education Institutions." Paper presented at the annual meeting of the American Educational Research Association, New Orleans, La., Apr. 2002.

Smith, K. M. "The Impact of College on White Students' Racial Attitudes." Paper presented at the annual forum of the Association for Institutional Research, Chicago, May 1993.

Springer, L., and others. "Attitudes Toward Campus Diversity: Participation in a Racial or Cultural Awareness Workshop." *Review of Higher Education*, 1996, *20*(1), 53–68.

Taylor, S. H. "The Impact of College on the Development of Tolerance." *NASPA Journal*, 1998, *35*, 281–295.

Terenzini, P. T., Springer, L., Pascarella, E. T., and Nora, A. "Academic and Out-of-Class Influences on Students' Intellectual Orientations." *Review of Higher Education*, 1995, *19*(1), 23–44.

Terenzini, P. T., and Upcraft, M. L. "Assessing Program and Service Outcomes." In M. L. Upcraft and J. H. Schuh (eds.), *Assessment in Student Affairs: A Guide for Practitioners.* San Francisco: Jossey-Bass, 1996.

Whitt, E. J., and others. "Influences on Students' Openness to Diversity and Challenge in the Second and Third Years of College." *Journal of Higher Education,* 2001, 72, 172–204.

ELLEN M. BROIDO is assistant professor of higher education and student affairs at Bowling Green State University in Ohio.

ROBERT D. REASON is assistant professor of education and professor-in-charge of the college student affairs program at Penn State University. He is also a research associate in Penn State's Center for the Study of Higher Education.

3

This chapter explores obstacles to and strategies for developing social justice attitudes and actions with men.

Increasing Men's Development of Social Justice Attitudes and Actions

Tracy L. Davis, Rachel Wagner

> After hundreds of years of anti-racist struggle, more than ever before non-white people are currently calling attention to the primary role white people must play in anti-racist struggle. The same is true of the struggle to eradicate sexism—men have a primary role to play.
>
> —bell hooks (2004)

Working with social justice issues, in our experience, is not for the faint of heart. Power, privilege, and difference constantly permeate working and personal relationships. Having the courage to surface the dynamics in play, having the energy and motivation to struggle with and struggle through learning curves, and finally having care and respect for one another throughout the process are hearty, albeit minimum, requirements.

As we wrote this chapter, we found ourselves engaged in a disagreement about the definitions of some terms. Probing further beneath differences of opinion, we found that philosophically, we were entering the conversation at different points: one voice female and subordinated, one voice male and privileged. Despite our love and respect for each other as friends and colleagues, identities and social realities exist to complicate our interactions, pulling at us with their loyalties or urging us to reconstruct the discussion to fit our existing mental frameworks.

Different emotions surfaced—confusion, annoyance, disappointment, urgency—and at some point each of us noticed that we were replicating the discussion of our chapter. We were each struggling with the need to have our social and cultural experiences validated and understood. We were shut

New Directions for Student Services, no. 110, Summer 2005 © Wiley Periodicals, Inc.

down or tuned out at points, disengaging from the discussion to seek support from others who shared our experience. At all times, however, we were committed to the experience; we found ourselves turning away from what we were not willing to believe or do, and instead turning toward what we could imagine and envision. And our result, a new shared definition of both the terminology in question and our relationship, was worth every effort, every tear imaginable, much as is the goal of male ally development.

In this chapter we discuss concepts, models, and research related to men's development in order to provide a framework for promoting social justice attitudes and actions with male students. We begin by discussing barriers to ally development with men. In addition to barriers related to internalized privilege, we add men's adherence to hegemonic masculinity and a culture of misunderstanding related to men's contradictory experiences of power. By deconstructing the complexities of each obstacle, suggestions emerge for effectively engaging men in a developmental journey toward attitudes and actions consistent with social justice. We also offer explicit strategies for addressing developmental barriers.

Barriers to Ally Development

Barriers to developing social justice attitudes and actions in men are rooted in both internal processes and external influences. While it may be tempting, particularly in a culture that values individualism (see the discussion of the social construction of identity in Chapter One, this volume), to simply hold men individually accountable for patriarchal sexism, doing so risks ignoring the construction of self through negotiation with larger cultural scripts such as hegemonic masculinity. This in no way diminishes men's oppression of women or the responsibility men have for challenging patriarchal privilege. Rather, it suggests that men are also harmed by patriarchy through the manufactured consent to hegemonic standards. Critiquing the manufactured hegemonic messages offers insight into effective strategies for promoting social justice attitudes and actions in men. That is, helping men understand that they both benefit from and are harmed by patriarchy can provide motivation for understanding and the development of social justice perspectives.

Believing that men are harmed is not always an easy hurdle to jump. For example, hooks (2004) argued that "women active in the feminist movement have not wanted to focus in any way on male pain so as not to deflect attention away from the focus on male privilege" (p. 558). While this is understandable, focusing exclusively on the benefits of male privilege may not only ignore how men experience reality, but it may also inadvertently inhibit male students from effectively developing social justice attitudes. We clarify this argument through the following discussion of the complex intersections of men's privilege, men's adherence to restricted gender role scripts, and subsequently what Kaufman (1999) called "men's contradictory experience of power" (p. 59).

Privilege. In a patriarchy, men are afforded certain liberties while women face restrictions. The liberties are institutionalized to construct male privilege, while restrictions serve to oppress women. Subordination permeates the experience of women, but male privilege often goes unacknowledged by men. As McIntosh (2001) persuasively illustrated, unearned advantages (since they are unearned) are easily overlooked as a form of privilege. For example, Johnson (1997) writes:

> When I go out at night for a walk alone . . . I rarely think about how the mere fact of my being male grants me the freedom to move about with relatively little fear in a world that is far more threatening and frightening for women. The fact that I don't consciously *feel* privileged isn't because I'm not privileged. In part it's because my privilege consists of otherwise unremarkable aspects of everyday life. Being able to take a late night walk by myself simply because I feel like it or need a quart of milk isn't the kind of thing that makes me feel privileged. But it is a privilege when a society is organized in ways that systematically deny it to some while allowing it for others [p. 177].

Supporting the idea that male privilege often goes unacknowledged, a recent study by one of us found that male college students did not often think about themselves as men (Davis, 2002). In fact, when asked, "What is it like to be a man on this campus?" men generally responded with silence and confusion. This reaction is unsurprising given the nature of privilege. Privilege essentially allows men to go about their lives without having to think about the impact of sexism on women.

Unacknowledged privilege is a considerable barrier for promoting social justice attitudes and actions with men for several reasons. As illustrated by Bishop's (2002) model in Chapter Two (this volume), becoming an ally first requires an understanding of how oppression works. The invisible experience of privilege serves both to facilitate denial that oppression even exists and inhibit a more complex and empathic understanding of oppression for those who intellectually understand it. That is, those who have a purely or even predominantly intellectualized experience (as opposed to a firsthand personal experience) with oppression may not fully see oppression for what it is or have a more difficult time sustaining social justice attitudes and actions in the face of challenge.

One of the "disadvantages of the advantages" of privilege (A. Berkowitz, personal communication to T. Davis, March 2002) is that it may also inhibit identity development and a more mature understanding of self in relation to the multicultural world. According to Marcia (1966), identity develops through a series of crises and subsequent commitments. Essentially those failing to struggle with identity issues find themselves in the less developmentally complex and less mature foreclosed status. Since male privilege inhibits men from understanding themselves as men, understanding oneself as a person with multiple dimensions of identity is not even experienced as a developmental task. In this manner, many men remain at the naive stage of the Hardiman and Jackson (1992) social identity development model discussed in Chapter Two (this volume). To acquire a redefined or internalized stage where critical examination and growth can occur, critical incidents are key. According to many identity theories, critical incidents (such as experiences of racism) are a crucial precipitator of growth. Those who are privileged seldom experience critical incidents or, if they do, can more readily use their privilege to avoid or reduce the severity of the consequences.

A third reason that privilege can provide a serious obstacle to the development of social justice actions in men is the lack of environmental incentive for change. By definition, social justice allies join with others to work toward ending oppression of others, but they also must work toward their own liberation (Bishop, 2002). Those with privilege who are unaware of oppression, however, see nothing that needs liberating. In fact, one does not have to do a thing to preserve the status quo of privilege. As a result, there are few apparent external incentives or environmental presses for men to combat oppression. As we illustrate later in this chapter, however, both men and women are hurt by sexism.

Men's Adherence to Hegemonic Masculinity. Men, like women, negotiate gendered social scripts. According to Kimmel and Messner (2004), "Our identity as men is developed through a complex process of interaction with the culture in which we both learn the gender scripts appropriate to our culture and attempt to modify those scripts to make them more palatable" (p. xv). For men, the gender scripts include restrictive emotionality (big boys don't cry); socialized control, power, and competition (be a take-charge man); restrictive sexual and affectionate behavior among men (don't be vulnerable, particularly with another man); and obsession with achievement, work, and success (worth measured according to title and income) (O'Neil and others, 1986).

The sex role scripts for men can serve to inhibit development of social justice attitudes and actions. For example, men are socialized to fear, deny, and even attack "feminine attributes" in themselves and others (Kimmel and Messner, 2004; Klindlon and Thompson, 2000; O'Neil and others, 1986; Pollack, 1998). In fact, according to Kaufman (1999), "The acquisition of hegemonic (and most subordinate) masculinities is a process through which men come to suppress a range of emotions, needs, and possibilities such as nurturing, receptivity, empathy, and compassion which are experienced as inconsistent with the power of manhood" (p. 65).

It seems obvious that denied attributes like empathy and receptivity are related to, if not critical for, the development of social justice attitudes and actions. Klindlon and Thompson (2000), moreover, illustrated the connection between denied emotions and social justice attitudes when they stated that hegemonic masculinity "imposes a code of silence on boys, requiring them to suffer without speaking of it and to be silent witness to acts of cruelty to others. . . . To remain silent is strong and masculine, and to speak out is not" (Klindlon and Thompson, 2000, p. 92). Empathy for the experience of others, a care orientation, and "speaking out" in response to pain are characteristics both outside the traditional male role and also vital to the development of social justice attitudes and actions.

Another aspect of hegemonic masculinity that may have an adverse impact on the development of social justice attitudes relates to toughness and vulnerability. Pollack (1998) suggested that according to the "boy code," male expression of vulnerability is taboo. Essentially men are taught to "take it like a man" and view complaining and expressions of outrage as whining. An understanding of oppression and development of social justice attitudes requires, however, awareness that some people are targeted and victimized, while some people benefit and are privileged. Thus, according to hegemonic masculinity, even expressions of legitimate outrage growing out of experiences of oppression can be seen as whining.

Hegemonic masculinity and male privilege coalesce to provide powerful barriers to the development of social justice attitudes and action. To the privileged, where experiences of oppressive treatment are largely absent, it simply rings true that people get what they deserve. Moreover, men are taught that if people are complaining about the way they are being treated, it is because they are whiners who violate the boundaries of traditional masculinity.

Men's Contradictory Experiences of Power. In addition to privilege and men's adherence to hegemonic masculinity, Kaufman (1999) suggested that men's experience of power as a paradox is confusing to most men. This confusion, if left unarticulated and unrecognized, can be a source of obstruction in men's development of social justice attitudes and actions. The paradox of masculinity is that "in objective social analysis, men as a group have power over women as a group: but in their subjective experience of the world, men as individuals do not feel powerful. In fact, they feel powerless" (Capraro, 2004, p. 192). This is not a denial of privilege. As illustrated earlier, privilege exists whether or not it is felt or recognized. Essentially men's contradictory experiences of power suggest that men's social power is both the source of individual privilege and also the source of individual experience of pain and alienation.

One example of men's contradictory experience of power is related to the complexities of social identity development articulated in the Jones and McEwen (2000) model of multiple dimensions of identity outlined in Chapter One (this volume). For example, the experience of men with power and privilege is based on a range of social identities: gay male, African American male, Jewish male, effeminate male, working-class male, and so forth. According to Kaufman (1999), "The social power of a poor man is different than a rich one, a working class black man from a working class white man, a gay man from a bisexual man from a straight man, a Jewish man in Ethiopia from a Jewish man in Israel, a teenage boy from an adult" (p. 68).

It is important to clarify that we do not deny that men as a group enjoy social power or even that men within their subgroups tend to have power and privilege. To the contrary, we are acknowledging crucial complexities related to multiple dimensions of identity that describe power and power-lessness on a continuum rather than a binary opposite. hooks (2004) captured men's paradoxical experience of power when she claimed:

> The poor or working class man who has been socialized via sexist ideology to believe that there are privileges and powers he should possess solely because he is male often finds that few if any of these benefits are automatically bestowed him in life. More than any other male group in the United States, he is constantly concerned about the contradiction between the notion of masculinity he was taught and his inability to live up to that notion. He is usually "hurt," emotionally scarred because he does not have the privilege or power society has taught him "real men" should possess. Alienated, frustrated, pissed off, he may attack, abuse and oppress an individual woman or women, but he is not reaping positive benefits from his support and perpetuation of sexist ideology [p. 559].

Moreover, according to hooks, "if the feminist movement ignores his predicament, dismisses his hurt, or writes him off as just another male enemy, then we are passively condoning his actions" (p. 559).

Barriers to promoting development of social justice attitudes and actions with men do not disappear once the complexities of men's contradictory experiences of power are recognized. In fact, ironically, another barrier can be constructed. The barrier is related to important distinctions between harm and subordination and between individual pain and institutional oppression. In student affairs work, the barrier can be constructed by individuals who believe that men's contradictory experiences of power mean that men are oppressed just as women are *or* by individuals who believe that men are not harmed by the patriarchy. The former inappropriately equates individual discrimination or harm with the institutional web of oppression, and the latter dismisses men's contradictory experience of power (that is, men's experience). Men are simultaneously privileged and harmed by their experiences of power. In other words, as a group, men are the recipients of power and privilege, but as individuals, they often fall short of hegemonic masculinity and experience the pain associated with it. The relationship between men's privilege and pain offers insight into strategies to promote social justice attitudes and actions in men.

Strategies for Promoting Growth

The obstacles to growth related to privilege, adherence to hegemonic masculinity, and men's contradictory experiences of power must be understood and used to guide developmental interventions. Each identified barrier provides clues for working with men to promote attitudes and actions consistent with social justice. In this section, we offer strategies that directly address the barriers discussed earlier in this chapter.

Strategies Related to Privilege. Since privilege associated with being a man is unearned and often unacknowledged, a first step toward promoting understanding necessary for development of social justice attitudes is to find ways to help men acknowledge their privilege. McIntosh's discussion (2001) of the nature of privilege is a powerful tool for making the invisible aspects of privilege visible. Student affairs faculty and professionals should consider using this reading when appropriate. The specific examples of privilege that McIntosh shares can be used as a model for questions that professionals might ask themselves and the students with whom they work.

Privilege "step-forward" or "stand-up" group exercises can also be effective for raising unacknowledged privilege to awareness. Participants are asked to begin shoulder to shoulder on a line. Questions are then raised by the facilitator, the answers to which will lead participants to either step forward (privilege) or step back (oppression). A sample question is, "If you were ever uncomfortable about a joke related to your race, ethnicity, gender, or sexual orientation but felt unsafe to confront the situation, take one step back." (A full copy of this exercise is available at http://www.msu.edu/~bailey22/Privilege_Exercise.htm.)

Student affairs professionals who promote learning and growth outside the classroom with individual men must challenge them to see that they have a gender, sex, race, and other dimensions of identity that may be currently experienced as invisible. Chickering and Reisser's theory (1993) clearly distinguishes identity as a central developmental task for traditional-aged college students. One's sex and gender are certainly important aspects of identity. Especially in the light of Davis's research (2002) that suggests men did not think about themselves as men, masculinity appears to be an important aspect of men's identity that needs to be intentionally raised. If it is not personally evaluated, hegemonic masculinity will certainly develop deeper roots. Just as Helms (1992) reminded us that white people have a race, men have a sex and gender. Once on the developmental map, the meanings of sex and gender, what one has learned about being a man, can be reconsidered in the light of the social construction of identities. The social identity concept that society has something to say about who men are and who they should be can lead to important discoveries about the nature of oppression and privilege. The Counseling Center at Bowling Green State University, for example, offers a Men's Issues Brown Bag Series aimed at exploring men's sex role socialization.

Another strategy is to establish men's studies courses focusing on social justice. As mentioned in Chapter Two (this volume), Broido's research (2000) suggested that the structure of an academic class was a key component of ally development. Ironically, some have been opposed to men's studies curriculum out of fear that it somehow takes away from or is inconsistent with women's studies. Men's studies, however, need not be viewed simply as "male enlightenment," but rather can be construed as having the same goals as feminism. Brod (1987) illustrated how men's studies can put privilege at the center of attention as opposed to leaving it unacknowledged when he wrote, "Leaving men's lives unexamined leaves male privilege unexamined, and hence more powerful. . . . The most important boon granted by men's studies is therefore female *empowerment*, reached through greater knowledge of the dominant group" (p. 272).

Strategies Related to Hegemonic Masculinity. Conceiving identity as socially constructed offers fertile ground for growth in terms of the kind of self-understanding and knowledge about oppression necessary for the development of social justice attitudes. As men reflect on the gender role scripts they have been sold, they can begin to ask questions related to messages, who is sending them, and to what ends. Josselson (1996) illustrated that "identity is better understood as not just a private, individual matter . . . [but] a complex negotiation between the person and society" (p. 31).

Equipped with this knowledge, student affairs professionals can design courses and programs aimed at asking students to evaluate gender role scripts in commercials, sit-coms, movies, magazine ads, and other cultural transmitters. As students evaluate the messages, themes about who men and women are "supposed to be" emerge, and the reality that some, if not most, people cannot meet hegemonic standards enters awareness. The process of understanding who is harmed and who benefits from various messages provides some building blocks for establishing a more complex understanding of one's privileges, one's disadvantages, and the more sophisticated web of institutional oppression that are important for the development of social justice attitudes.

Interventions can also be constructed using the gender role conflict theoretical framework of O'Neil and his colleagues (1986) discussed earlier. For example, Davis (2000) uses contemporary sit-coms and entertainment media to illustrate gender role conflict themes, and challenges participants to view messages they receive about being a man more critically and make their own decisions in spite of cultural press. Career development professionals can focus on men's obsession with achievement, work, and success; residence life staff can offer all-male sexual assault prevention programs consistent with socialized control and power; Greek life professionals can open discussions with fraternity men about the impact of gender role conflict on how, which, and under what conditions emotions are expressed and relationships developed. All of these examples ask students to consider the messages they have learned, evaluate whether the messages are consistent with their self-image, and essentially make choices about whether to keep or discard (that is, to self-construct) attributes that make up their identity. Emotions denied men by hegemonic masculinity (nurturance, receptivity, empathy, and compassion) can be explored and reevaluated, which can serve to reduce resistance to ideas congruent with social justice.

In terms of facilitating discussion with men, Pollack (2001) offered the following strategies: create a safe space, give men time to feel comfortable with expression, seek out and provide alternative pathways for expression (that is, relate while engaging in action-oriented activities), listen without judging, avoid shaming, and give affirmation and affection. In terms of working with those who are privileged, our own experiences of subordination and pain or our own needs for social justice may lead us away from these fundamental professional discussion guidelines. For example, one who has experienced the pain of oppression may transfer reactionary emotions like anger onto privileged identities. Such reaction may provoke defensiveness and reactions that inhibit learning and violate the central obligation of an educator.

Strategies Related to Men's Contradictory Experiences of Power. It is important to note that even the most apparently privileged man experiences some level of pain related to hegemonic standards of masculinity. Kaufman (1999) argued, for example, that the needs and feelings that are deemed inconsistent with masculinity result in enormous pain and fear. This is a critical point. If men are not simply the agents of oppression (although this is one dimension) but also affected negatively by it, men's investment in change takes on new meaning. Men's pain can be a vehicle for initiating awareness about, developing understanding for, and ultimately promoting action related to social justice. Student affairs professionals need to seriously examine the potential of the paradox of men's experience of power for promoting social justice attitudes.

Once again, it may be important to clarify that focusing on men's pain is not aimed at ignoring men's privilege or diminishing the oppression of women. As hooks (2004) suggested, it may be difficult for those who have experienced subordination and who live within the web of oppression

> to hear emphasis placed on men being victimized by sexism; they cling to the "all men are the enemy" version of reality. . . . While it in no way diminishes the seriousness of male abuse and oppression of women, or negates male responsibility for exploitive actions, the pain men experience can serve as a catalyst calling attention to the need for change [p. 558].

For men who have identity dimensions that are targeted (for example, Jewish men, gay men, black men), it may be much easier to promote understanding about the realities of oppression but somewhat harder for them to accept the privileges associated with being a man. The multiple dimensions of identity model (Jones and McEwen, 2000) discussed in Chapter One (this volume) is a useful framework for facilitating understanding about the complex interaction among various identity dimensions and the shifting contexts that are related to individual experiences of privilege or oppression. Interventions incorporating the concepts in this model should resonate with students' experiences and can promote discussion beyond an oversimplified dualistic conception of oppression. Kaufman (1999) even claimed that "our whole language of oppression is in need of overhaul for it is based on simple binary oppositions, reductionist equations between identity and social location, and unifocal notions of self" (p. 70).

Strategies for Men to Become Allies to Women. For men, understanding privilege, hegemonic masculinity, and their own contradictory experiences of power is fundamental to developing an antisexist or profeminist identity and engaging in social justice attitudes and actions. Working to interrupt sexism cannot rely solely on the work of women. Being an ally to women means interrupting sexism in its various forms. On an individual level, it often means challenging statements or behaviors that serve to circumscribe the roles and choices available to women. On an institutional level, it means, for example, serving as an advocate on issues related to pay equity, representation, promotion to leadership, and harassment-free environments.

Removing sexist practice, sexist language, and sexist attitudes is vital; however, removing oppressive behavior is inadequate. Sex- and gender-related social justice is not simply the absence of sexism; it is cultivating understanding, honoring human differences, and mindfully taking action. Men and women must envision our destination and make a commitment to it. What replaces sexist practices, attitudes, and language? What other ways of engaging can we enact as a liberated community? The answers to these questions should also be part of our conversations. The following three areas can help guide men's efforts in serving as allies to women and move the discourse toward what replaces current practice.

"In the moment" action aimed at acknowledging privilege when it is conferred and oppression when it is overlooked is one way men can address sexism. Law (2000) provides powerful, tangible examples of actions men can incorporate into daily interactions, as well as questions men can ask for self and group reflection. Law lists a variety of traditional ways of thinking that men can challenge, from dominating conversations to air-time and interruptions, to seeking out women's opinions that agreed with their own, rather than listening to differing opinions. As discussed earlier in this chapter, men are afforded privileges they have not requested. In a meeting, a man's point of view may be taken more seriously than a woman's. A man may not be able to force the participants to take him less seriously or the woman more so; however, he can surface the dynamic he suspects is operating, by saying, for example, "I don't think we really listened to Nicola's position. I noticed that when Micah repeated it, he was given credit." Noticing when this happens and naming it provides a unique opportunity for deconstructing a system that otherwise continues unquestioned and becomes normalized.

Learning about the nature of violence is a second critical engagement for men. Violence and the threat of violence are key factors in enforcing the patriarchy. Physical, emotional, and economic violence occurs between the powerful and the powerless, including other men, women, animals, and the natural world. Working to end violence in all forms is necessary. Men can also join or form groups to educate other men about violence against women and children. Effective programs will not reinforce hegemonic masculinity and the notion that men need to protect or save women.

Finally, becoming an ally to women means engaging men in reflecting about the ways the feminine is denigrated in both women and men. Hegemonic masculinity—that which is celebrated and imposed by most aspects of social experience and popular culture—has to be individually reexamined. Male faculty, administrators, and staff can role-model rejection of hegemonic principles and engagement of multiple or alternative masculinities, providing options to young men who are bombarded with messages of dominance and control as defining manhood. Males working in career development, for example, can also serve to help female students explore possibilities that are consistent with the student's values, interests, and abilities as opposed to only those careers consistent with traditional gender roles.

Conclusion

As difficult as it may be, student affairs professionals should remember that "despite the privileges White men receive and become accustomed to, men often feel like workhorses and many are ill-equipped to comfortably experience and express a full range of emotions such as fear, depression, and uncertainty" (Scott and Robinson, 2001, p. 416). The emotions denied men as a result of hegemonic masculinity may be key to the often locked doors that keep the development of social justice attitudes and actions outside men's experience. The pain associated with such denial and the corresponding privilege conferred to men by patriarchy provide crucial clues for promoting the growth and development of attitudes consistent with social justice.

If student affairs professionals want to effectively engage college men and promote development of social justice attitudes and actions, they need to understand the barriers related to privilege, hegemonic masculinity, and men's contradictory experiences of power. Strategies consistent with the concepts associated with these barriers should be more effective than those that rely on more conceptually simplistic understandings of men and masculinities. While student affairs professionals in general have an obligation to promote growth and development responsibly, men have a particularly important role to play. As hooks (2004) reminded us, "Since men are the primary agents maintaining and supporting sexism and sexist oppression, they can only be successfully eradicated if men are compelled to assume responsibility for transforming their consciousness and the consciousness of society as a whole" (p. 563).

References

Bishop, A. *Becoming an Ally: Breaking the Cycle of Oppression in People.* (2nd ed.) Halifax, Nova Scotia: Fernwood, 2002.

Brod, H. "A Case for Men's Studies." In M. S. Kimmel (ed.), *Changing Men: New Directions in Research on Men and Masculinity.* Thousand Oaks, Calif.: Sage, 1987.

Broido, E. M. "The Development of Social Justice Allies During College: A Phenomenological Investigation." *Journal of College Student Development,* 2000, *41,* 3–18.

Capraro, R. L. "Why College Men Drink: Alcohol, Adventure, and the Paradox of Masculinity." In M. S. Kimmel and M. A. Messner (eds.), *Men's Lives.* (6th ed.) Needham Heights, Mass.: Allyn and Bacon, 2004.

Chickering, A. W., and Reisser, L. *Education and Identity.* San Francisco: Jossey-Bass, 1993.

Davis, T. L. "Programming for Men to Reduce Sexual Violence." In D. Liddell and J. Lund (eds.), *Powerful Programming for Student Learning: Approaches That Make a Difference.* New Directions for Student Services, no. 90. San Francisco: Jossey-Bass, 2000.

Davis, T. L. "Voices of Gender Role Conflict: The Social Construction of College Men's Identity." *Journal of College Student Development,* 2002, *43*(4), 508–521.

Hardiman, R., and Jackson, B. W. "Racial Identity Development: Understanding Racial Dynamics in College Classrooms and on Campus." In M. Adams (ed.), *Promoting Diversity in College Classrooms: Innovative Responses for the Curriculum, Faculty, and Institution.* New Directions for Teaching and Learning, no. 52. San Francisco: Jossey-Bass, 1992.

Helms, J. E. *A Race Is a Nice Thing to Have: A Guide to Being a White Person or Understanding the White Persons in Your Life.* Topeka, Kans.: Content Communications, 1992.

hooks, b. "Men: Comrades in Struggle." In M. S. Kimmel and M. A. Messner (eds.), *Men's Lives.* (6th ed.). Needham Heights, Mass.: Allyn and Bacon, 2004.

Johnson, A. G. *The Gender Knot: Unraveling Our Patriarchal Legacy.* Philadelphia: Temple University Press, 1997.

Jones, S. R., and McEwen, M. K. "A Conceptual Model of Multiple Dimensions of Identity." *Journal of College Student Development,* 2000, *41*(4), 405–414.

Josselson, R. *Revising Herself: The Story of Women's Identity from College to Midlife.* New York: Oxford University Press, 1996.

Kaufman, M. "Men, Feminism, and Men's Contradictory Experiences of Power." In J. A. Kuypers (ed.), *Men and Power.* Halifax, Nova Scotia: Fernwood Books, 1999.

Kimmel, M. S., and Messner, M. A. (eds.). *Men's Lives.* (6th ed.) Needham Heights, Mass.: Allyn and Bacon, 2004.

Klindlon, D. J., and Thompson, M. *Raising Cain: Protecting the Emotional Life of Boys.* New York: Ballantine Books, 2000.

Law, I. "Adopting the Principle of Pro-Feminism." In M. Adams and others (eds.), *Readings for Diversity and Social Justice.* New York: Routledge, 2000.

Marcia, J. E. "Development and Validation of Ego-Identity Status." *Journal of Personality and Social Psychology,* 1966, *5,* 551–558.

McIntosh, P. "White Privilege and Male Privilege: A Personal Account of Coming to See Correspondences Through Work in Women's Studies." In M. L. Andersen and P. Hill Collins (eds.), *Race, Class, and Gender: An Anthology.* Belmont, Calif.: Wadsworth, 2001.

O'Neil, J. M., and others. "Gender Role Conflict Scale: College Men's Fear of Femininity." *Sex Roles,* 1986, *14*(5–6), 335–350.

Pollack, W. S. *Real Boys: Rescuing Our Sons from the Myths of Boyhood.* New York: Holt, 1998.

Pollack, W. S. *Real Boys Workbook: The Definitive Guide to Understanding and Interacting with Boys of All Ages.* New York: Villard, 2001.

Scott, D. A., and Robinson, T. L. "White Male Identity Development: The Key Model." *Journal of Counseling and Development,* 2001, 79, 415–421.

TRACY L. DAVIS is an associate professor of college student personnel and program coordinator in the educational and interdisciplinary studies department at Western Illinois University.

RACHEL WAGNER is a doctoral candidate in social justice education at the University of Massachusetts, Amherst.

The authors discuss strategies for the development of heterosexual allies and actions that allies can take to support this social identity group.

Encouraging the Development of Social Justice Attitudes and Actions in Heterosexual Students

Nancy J. Evans, Ellen M. Broido

While issues facing lesbian, gay, bisexual, and transgender (LGBT) individuals have become more visible in recent years, so has the backlash against the steps that have been taken to afford equal rights to LGBT people. Given the current climate, heterosexual allies are critically important in the fight for social justice. The complexity of and need for ally work are evident in many ways. One of these was our realization, on reviewing initial drafts of this volume, that only in this chapter did we not address our own social identities. While I, Ellen, am completely out in my professional and personal lives, I believe this is the first time I have explicitly identified myself as lesbian in a professional publication. It is surprisingly challenging. I, Nancy, identify as a heterosexual ally but do not often share that identity in writing either. Both of us share a long history of activism for LGBT rights and efforts to foster the development of LGBT allies.

Throughout the chapter, we use both the abbreviations *LGB* and *LGBT*. Transgender issues are included where addressed in the literature and where the issues of lesbian, gay, and bisexual people intersect with those of transgender people. However, we acknowledge that the issues are far from synonymous, and discrimination based on sexual orientation is not the same as discrimination based on gender identity or expression. While conventionally gendered people, heterosexual or LGB, can act as allies for transgender people, we do not specifically address those issues in this chapter. This is an important topic, and we hope others will expand on this work to develop specific ally interventions for the transgender population.

In this chapter, we introduce several models of heterosexual identity development and present research findings identifying factors that influence the attitudes that heterosexual individuals hold about LGB individuals and how negative attitudes can be changed. We review strategies that have been effective in the development of heterosexual allies and actions that allies can take to support LGBT individuals.

Heterosexual Identity Development

Mohr (2002) argued that understanding one's heterosexual identity is necessary to develop affirmative attitudes toward LGB individuals. However, as Bieschke (2002) pointed out, because heterosexuality is assumed to be normative while all other sexual identities are considered deviant, heterosexuality is rarely viewed as a social identity, and the privileges that are associated with this dominant identity are taken for granted. In the early part of the twentieth century, Freud suggested that heterosexuality is a constructed identity. However, most theorists who followed Freud rejected his ideas, taking an essentialist position that heterosexuality is innate and fixed (Eliason, 1995).

It was not until the late 1960s that theorists again called attention to the roles that society and culture play in shaping individuals' beliefs about who they are as sexual beings (see, for example, Macintosh, 1981; Wilkinson and Kitzinger, 1993). Feminist writers stressed that a heterosexual orientation is assumed in society and pointed out the powerful social forces directing women toward a heterosexual identity (Hyde and Jaffee, 2000). Taking a developmental approach based on Marcia's theory of identity development (1980), Eliason (1995) examined essays in which heterosexual students wrote about how their sexual identity was formed and how it affected their lives. Most students appeared to have foreclosed identities in that they had unquestioningly accepted the heterosexual identity given to them by parents and society.

Sullivan (1998) modified Hardiman and Jackson's racial identity development model (1992) to describe both LGB and heterosexual identity. In her model, all individuals move through five stages of increasing awareness and complexity regarding their sexual identity. In the first stage, *naiveté,* heterosexual individuals have little awareness of sexual orientation. The next stage, *acceptance,* can be either passive, with individuals taking heterosexuality for granted, or active, with individuals more openly expressing and acting on negative opinions of homosexuality. Stage three, *resistance,* can also be passive or active. Passive resistance is characterized by recognition of heterosexism but also a belief that one can do nothing about it, while individuals in active resistance both acknowledge their own homophobic attitudes and confront those of others. The fourth stage, *redefinition,* involves establishment of a positive heterosexual identity defined by more than rejection of heterosexist beliefs. Individuals who are able to establish an identity independent of normative heterosexist definitions achieve the final stage of development, *internalization*.

Simoni and Walters (2001) also proposed that heterosexual identity development parallels white identity development. Similar to the model introduced by Sullivan (1998), Simoni and Walters described five stages moving from a complete lack of awareness of heterosexism to full acknowledgment of the heterosexual bias in society. In their study, older students, those in more advanced classes, and women exhibited greater awareness of heterosexism, while younger undergraduates, men, and people of color were less likely to acknowledge concern about the privilege accorded to heterosexuals.

Mohr (2002) suggested that heterosexual identity derives from the interaction of individuals' "working models of sexual orientation" (p. 539) and their "core motivations" (p. 539). Individuals' working models (beliefs) about heterosexual identity are determined by their personal experiences with sexuality and their exposure to information about sexual orientation. Mohr identified four working models of sexual orientation.

Similar to white individuals in Helms's Contact status (1995) of racial identity development who view themselves as color-blind, individuals using Mohr's first working model (2002), *democratic heterosexuality,* "tend to view people of all sexual orientations as essentially the same" (pp. 540–541). These individuals have not seriously considered their identity as heterosexual persons or reflected on the role that privilege and oppression play in the lives of individuals with different sexual orientations. The second working model, *compulsory heterosexuality,* is based on the belief that heterosexuality is the only appropriate sexual orientation. Individuals using this schema generally hold negative attitudes about LGB people and accept existing stereotypes. In *politicized heterosexuality,* Mohr's third working model, individuals focus on the privilege associated with their sexual orientation, often experiencing feelings of guilt, anger, and self-blame. They may view LGB people as heroic and push these individuals to "come out." In the final model, *integrative heterosexuality,* heterosexual individuals are aware that people of all sexual orientations are influenced by the oppressive system of which they are a part and realize that because of their heterosexual identity, they are accorded privileges that LGB people do not have.

Individuals' core motivations—to be accepted by others and to maintain an internally consistent self-concept—contribute to the manner in which they develop and live out their sexual identities (Mohr, 2002). Thus, individuals are influenced by both the views of significant others regarding sexual orientation and their own need for consistency "between their inner experiences of their heterosexuality and their social expression of their heterosexuality" (p. 548). Mohr suggested that individuals who find themselves in LGB-affirmative environments are influenced to develop a working model of sexual orientation consistent with those of people around them.

In the most comprehensive model of heterosexual identity development to date, Worthington, Savoy, Dillon, and Vernaglia (2002) defined heterosexual identity development as "the individual and social processes by which heterosexually identified persons acknowledge and define their sexual needs, values, sexual expression, and characteristics of sexual partners" (p. 510). In addition, they saw heterosexual identity development as based on an understanding of the privilege and oppression associated with majority and minority group status and including corresponding attitudes, values, and beliefs about LGB individuals.

Paralleling Fassinger and her colleagues' model of lesbian and gay identity formation (Fassinger, 1998), Worthington, Savoy, Dillon, and Vernaglia (2002) identified two interacting processes of heterosexual identity development: an individual process related to determination of personal sexual needs, values, and preferences and a social process centering around recognition of majority group membership as well as attitudes about LGB people. Movement through each of these processes is influenced by biological, social, and psychological factors.

Worthington, Savoy, Dillon, and Vernaglia (2002) proposed five developmental statuses applicable to both individual and group heterosexual identity. The first status is *unexplored commitment,* a sexual identity based on the assumptions and desires of significant others and society accepted without conscious thought or reflection, similar to Marcia's foreclosed identity status (1980); individuals are minimally aware of their dominant group membership and usually hold negative attitudes toward those who are lesbian, gay, or bisexual. *Active exploration,* the second status, is the position of those in the process of considering their sexual needs, values, and preferred activities; this status is similar to Marcia's moratorium identity status. At the group level, the individual begins to question the privilege automatically associated with a heterosexual identity and holds somewhat more positive attitudes toward LGB persons. *Diffusion,* the third status, also parallels Marcia's identity status in which individuals are engaged in neither exploration nor commitment. Individuals in this status may be actively rejecting the heterosexual behavior and identity mandated by others but have no specific self-chosen identity to replace what they have given up. The fourth status, *deepening and commitment,* is similar to identity achievement in Marcia's model, although it may be possible to enter without active exploration because of the strong norms in our society that prescribe a very narrow range of acceptable sexual behaviors and attitudes. Persons become more consciously aware of and actively choose both their individual and group sexual identities in this status, as well as their attitudes toward LGB individuals, which can be hostile, affirming, or somewhere between these extremes. The final status, *synthesis,* is the most complex, flexible, and congruent in that "individual sexual identity, group membership identity, and attitudes toward sexual minorities merge into an overall self-concept, which is conscious, volitional, and (hopefully) enlightened" (Worthington, Savoy, Dillon, and Vernaglia, 2002, p. 519).

The models of Mohr (2002) and Worthington, Savoy, Dillon, and Vernaglia (2002) have yet to be empirically tested. Thus, the implications of these models for the development of social justice allies are necessarily tentative. However, research findings (Eliason, 1995; Simoni and Walters, 2001) have supported Worthington, Savoy, Dillon, and Vernaglia's hypothesis that the extent of active exploration of and commitment to a heterosexual identity is related to awareness of sexual orientation issues and positive attitudes toward LGB people. Based on these findings, it appears that a first step in the development of the positive attitudes necessary to become an ally to LGB individuals is exploration of one's own sexual identity.

Mohr's model (2002) suggests that LGB-affirmative environments are influential in shaping positive working models of heterosexual orientation. Being around others who are secure in their sexual identity and affirmative of sexual diversity provides the necessary context and motivation for the self-exploration and commitment that Worthington, Savoy, Dillon, and Vernaglia (2002) have suggested as a precursor to achievement of a synthesized heterosexual identity. Thus, focusing on development of an affirmative environment in which social justice allies can explore and grow is important.

Attitudes and Attitude Change

The literature on heterosexual peoples' attitudes about nonheterosexual people is extensive. Over the past twenty years, a number of researchers have built on the foundational work of Herek (for example, 1986, 2000) to understand the demographic and personality traits associated with homophobia, heterosexism, and sexual prejudice. With a great deal of consistency, researchers have found that men hold beliefs and attitudes less accepting of lesbian, gay, and bisexual people than do women, and older people are less accepting than younger people. People with more fundamental religious values or greater attendance at religious services, those who live in the southern or midwestern United States or in rural areas, whose political ideology is conservative, who identify with the Republican party, who know fewer lesbian, gay, or bisexual people, who have fewer years of formal education, who have conventional beliefs about gender roles, and who score higher on measures of authoritarianism are all more likely than their counterparts to display greater sexual prejudice (Baslow and Johnson, 2000; Cotton-Huston and Waite, 2000; Herek, 2000). Clearly, a great deal is known about correlates of negative attitudes. What is missing, however, is substantial research into affirmative responses to LGBT people.

Forms and Functions of Attitudes About LGB People. Herek (1986) argued that people meet their own psychological needs by holding certain attitudes about other social groups. Attitudes can fulfill people's need to make sense of the world (referred to as *experiential* attitudes*)*, in which case their attitudes are largely based on their personal interactions with lesbian and gay people. Alternatively, people's attitudes about lesbians and gay men might serve to elicit some desired consequence that might arise from holding these values (*expressive* attitudes). In this case, people's attitudes actually have little to do with real gay and lesbian people, but instead serve as a vehicle for letting others know their values or identity, getting what they want or need from others, or avoiding anxiety. For example, a person might express a homophobic attitude to gain the respect of someone who also holds homophobic attitudes.

While Herek (1986) used this model to explain homophobic attitudes, his work implies some interesting strategies for fostering LGB-affirmative attitudes as well. Clearly, experiential attitudes will be influenced by contact with LGB people, and there is overwhelming evidence that contact with LBG people who are out, especially sustained or significant contact, is associated with more positive attitudes toward lesbians, bisexual people, and gay men (Bowen and Bourgeois, 2001; Haddock, Zanna, and Esses, 1993; Herek and Capitanio, 1996). Fostering interactions through experiences such as speakers' panels and creating environments in which it is safe for LBG people to be out will likely have an effect on heterosexuals' attitudes.

Possibly the greatest potential for influencing positive change in attitudes about LGB issues lies with peer groups. If significant peers express LGB-affirmative attitudes or if people become aware of the extent to which people they respect hold LBG-supportive beliefs, those whose attitudes about LGB people are based in expressive needs are likely to change their attitudes to receive affirmation from their peers. Another strategy, effective for those whose attitudes serve to reinforce their values or identity, is to highlight those aspects of their identity that are based in compassion, fairness, and equality.

Shifts in Social Attitudes Toward LGB People. Solid data are emerging that support the argument that social attitudes toward LGB people are changing, particularly among young people. Two questions about LGB issues have long been asked on the Higher Education Research Institution's survey of entering first-year students at colleges and universities across the United States. The researchers have documented increasingly positive attitudes toward lesbian and gay people over the past twenty-seven years ("Attitudes and Characteristics of Freshmen," 2001, 2002, 2003, 2004; Sax and others, 2001). In addition, Altemeyer (2001) found that Canadian college students' attitudes about LGB people, and to some extent their parents' attitudes, have become increasingly tolerant over the fourteen years of his research, with students tested in 1998 scoring in the "acceptance" range of the Attitudes Towards Homosexuals scale.

Altemeyer (2001) asked students what experiences had caused their attitudes about homosexuals to change. Students indicated the following experiences as having had the most positive effects: learning that there was a biological basis for homosexuality, knowing homosexual people, feeling sympathy for homosexuals after hearing about people beating them up, realizing that social attitudes toward homosexuals are becoming less condemning so that it is no longer a bad thing to accept them, and seeing respectable people associating with homosexuals. However, another study (Oldham and Kasser, 1999) found that students had mixed responses to learning that there may be a biological basis for homosexuality.

Changing Attitudes Toward LGBT People Through Programmatic Interventions. Over the past twenty years, educational institutions, as well as individuals and groups within those institutions, have attempted to develop interventions that would generate more accurate information about LGBT people and change students' attitudes and behaviors toward LGBT people. One of the most frequently used programs is the speakers' panel, in which several LGBT people, and sometimes heterosexual allies, speak to an audience (often students taking particular courses or students living in residence halls) about their life stories as LGBT people and as allies and respond to questions from the audience. There has been some research investigating the effects of these programs, with mixed findings. While two studies (Geasler, Croteau, Heineman, and Edlund, 1995; Nelson and Krieger, 1997) found that most students indicated more positive attitudes about lesbian and gay people after hearing a panel, Grutzeck and Gidycz (1997) suggested that the positive findings might have been a result of weaknesses in the design of the studies. They devised a study to overcome most of these limitations and found that hearing a gay and lesbian speakers' panel did not lead to attitudinal (as measured by pre- and posttests on two measures of attitudes toward homosexuals) or behavioral changes (as measured by willingness to speak to a prospective student who was gay or lesbian).

Iasenza and Troutt (1990) summarized another type of training program for student leaders designed to decrease intergroup prejudice related to ethnic, racial, and sexual differences. The three-hour program consisted of exercises allowing student leaders to explore their stereotypes and assumptions about nondominant group members and to engage in problem-solving activities related to scenarios involving prejudice. Participants developed an action plan to address prejudice throughout the academic year. Almost half of the students volunteered to form a committee to carry out this plan.

Some classroom interventions have proved to be effective in increasing awareness and changing attitudes. Eliason (1995) found that heterosexual students participating in a semester-long class, "Theorizing Sexual Identities," developed more positive attitudes about people with different sexual identities and became more aware of their own sexual identities. Simoni and Walters (2001) cautioned that didactic information, although helpful in changing attitudes, must be accompanied by experiential and cognitive components. One such activity, in which students were asked to wear a symbol, the pink triangle, which the Nazis in pre–World War II Germany required homosexuals to wear so they could be identified for persecution, was reported to be a very powerful learning experience when coupled with reflection, discussion, and provision of a theoretical context (Chesler and Zúniga, 1991).

As Mohr (2002) hypothesized, context has been found to be important in the development of self-reported positive attitudes and behaviors toward LGB people. Bieschke and Matthews (1996) found that an LGB-affirmative organizational climate was associated with low levels of homophobia among career counselors. Such a climate would be exemplified by inclusive policies, programming, hiring practices, visible symbols, and interpersonal interactions (Evans and Wall, 2000).

Developing Allies. Most research studies on attitude change have looked at reducing homophobia, but a few document success in creating advocates for LGBT people. Athanases and Larrabee (2003) studied the responses of ninety-seven teacher education students taking a course titled "Cultural Diversity and Education" at a public university in California. Stressing the importance of framing their teaching about gay and lesbian issues within a context of advocacy for all youth, the authors found that after reading materials about gay and lesbian students and teachers, and about the history of homophobia, and after hearing an out gay middle school teacher discuss his experiences, 47.4 percent of students gave written reactions indicating intentions to address gay and lesbian issues in their classrooms, confront homophobic language of their students and fellow teachers, provide information about lesbian and gay issues, and support lesbian and gay students and children of lesbian and gay parents. In this study, 28.9 percent indicated they saw a connection between heterosexism and homophobia and other forms of oppression, particularly racism and sexism. Similarly, Waterman, Reid, Garfield, and Hoy (2001) reported that heterosexual students who completed a course titled "Psychology of Homosexuality" were interested in providing support to LGBT individuals and left the class with significantly lower levels of homophobia. Students reported that the most effective teaching strategies in the class were guest speakers and movies.

Finkel, Storaasli, Bandele, and Schaefer (2003) reported the results of a study of graduate clinical and forensic psychology students who went through a mandatory training designed to increase knowledge about and support for LGBT people and issues. At the close of the training, participants were asked to list three LGBT-affirmative actions they intended to take over the next six months. While no assessment of the difficulty or significance of the intentions was made, after six months, 86.92 percent of the participants indicated that they had accomplished at least two of their intentions. The authors concluded that the training was an effective method of fostering an LGBT-affirming environment. Gelberg and Chojnacki (1995) reported that an intentional effort in a career counseling office to provide LGB-affirmative programming and resources also had the effect of increasing awareness among the counselors, resulting in their greater willingness to serve as allies for LGB students. Similarly, serving as investigators in an ethnographic study of the campus climate for LGBT students increased first-year students' awareness of oppression and contributed to their taking active ally roles in their living environments and other campus settings (Evans and Herriott, 2004).

Acting as Allies

Broido (2000) delineated three areas in which allies can contribute to the creation of an LGBT-affirmative campus environment: personal support, education of others, and institutional advocacy. Personal support takes various forms, including acceptance, support, and inclusiveness (Washington and Evans, 1991). Allies can demonstrate acceptance by interacting with LGBT individuals in a nonjudgmental and appreciative manner. Support includes actions such as confronting homophobic statements and standing up for the rights of LGBT people; attending programs sponsored by LGBT organizations; advocating for the inclusion of LBGT individuals in committees and decision-making bodies; and raising LGBT-related issues in classes, programs, and discussions. Inclusiveness involves use of nonexclusionary language (for example, *partner* or *significant other* rather than *husband* or *wife, boyfriend,* or *girlfriend*); appropriate representation of LGBT individuals in publications and other media; and recognition that not everyone is heterosexual (Washington and Evans, 1991).

In addition to showing support for LGBT individuals through their personal actions, allies take responsibility for educating others in a more formal manner (Washington and Evans, 1991). Education can take the form of programs and panel discussions designed to raise awareness of LGBT issues. Sponsoring speakers, movies, or plays on LGBT topics, as well as LGBT artists and musicians, are other forms of education.

Institutional advocacy is another important action allies can take (Broido, 2000). Such advocacy could include ensuring that LGBT student groups receive support and financial resources to function effectively, working to implement LGBT-inclusive nondiscrimination and antiharassment policies, advocating for domestic partner benefits, and stressing the need for LGBT-inclusive academic curricula. Allies can also advocate for hiring LGBT-affirmative staff and faculty and for the establishment of LGBT support services (Washington and Evans, 1991).

A number of campuses have developed formal ally programs to bring together like-minded students (Poynter, 2003). Ally groups support the efforts of LGBT student groups; initiate awareness programming; show visible support, such as placing ads in the campus newspaper; sponsor speakers and programs; provide a safe place for allies to come together to talk and share ideas; and develop ally training programs to assist others who are interested in supporting LGBT individuals. Often, ally organizations sponsor safe zone programs designed to provide a vehicle for allies to show their support of LGBT individuals by displaying visible symbols that they are safe people with whom to talk about LGBT-related concerns. These types of programs have been shown to have a powerful influence on raising awareness of LGBT issues on campus and creating an environment in which LGBT students and staff feel safer and more supported (Evans, 2002).

Conclusion

To combat the fear and ignorance at the heart of homophobia and heterosexism and create a world in which all people, regardless of their sexual orientation, are valued for who they are and the contributions they make, initiatives must be developed to increase awareness, change attitudes, and enhance knowledge and skills among heterosexual individuals. Research reviewed in this chapter has indicated that affirmative environments and programs that encourage self-exploration, provide opportunities for direct contact between LGB and heterosexual individuals, and combat stereotypes about LGB people can be successful in changing attitudes and helping heterosexual individuals develop LGB-affirmative heterosexual identities. However, taking the next step to become a heterosexual ally to LGBT people takes courage (Washington and Evans, 1991). Before students can be expected to engage in ally behaviors, student affairs professionals must take this step by educating themselves, creating LGBT-affirmative climates, and educating the students with whom they work. As role models, advocates, and change agents, student affairs professionals, along with the students they influence, can make a significant contribution toward creating a just and equitable environment for all students.

References

Altemeyer, B. "Changes in Attitudes Toward Homosexuals." *Journal of Homosexuality*, 2001, *42*, 63–75.

Athanases, S. Z., and Larrabee, T. G. "Toward a Consistent Stance in Teaching for Equity: Learning to Advocate for Lesbian- and Gay-Identified Youth." *Teaching and Teacher Education*, 2003, *19*, 237–261.

"Attitudes and Characteristics of Freshmen at Four-Year Colleges, Fall 2000." *Chronicle of Higher Education*, Aug. 31, 2001, p. 23.

"Attitudes and Characteristics of Freshmen at Four-Year Colleges, Fall 2001." *Chronicle of Higher Education*, Aug. 30, 2002, p. 26.

"Attitudes and Characteristics of Freshmen at Four-Year Colleges, Fall 2002." *Chronicle of Higher Education*, Aug. 29, 2003, p. 17.

"Attitudes and Characteristics of Freshmen at Four-Year Colleges, Fall 2003." *Chronicle of Higher Education*, Aug. 27, 2004, p. 19.

Baslow, S. A., and Johnson, K. "Predictors of Homophobia in Female College Students." *Sex Roles*, 2000, *41*, 391–404.

Bieschke, K. J. "Charting the Waters." *Counseling Psychologist*, 2002, *30*, 575–581.

Bieschke, K. J., and Matthews, C. "Career Counselor Attitudes and Behaviors Toward Gay, Lesbian, and Bisexual Clients." *Journal of Vocational Behavior*, 1996, *48*, 243–255.

Bowen, A. M., and Bourgeois, M. J. "Attitudes Toward Lesbian, Gay, and Bisexual College Students: The Contribution of Pluralistic Ignorance, Dynamic Social Impact, and Contact Theories." *Journal of American College Health,* 2001, *50*(2), 91–96.

Broido, E. M. "Ways of Being an Ally to Lesbian, Gay, and Bisexual Students." In V. A. Wall and N. J. Evans (eds.), *Toward Acceptance: Sexual Orientation Issues on Campus.* Lanham, Md.: American College Personnel Association, 2000.

Chesler, M. A., and Zúñiga, X. "Dealing with Prejudice and Conflict in the Classroom: The Pink Triangle Exercise." *Teaching Sociology,* 1991, *19,* 173–181.

Cotton-Huston, A., and Waite, B. "Anti-Homosexual Attitudes in College Students." *Journal of Homosexuality,* 2000, *38*(3), 117–133.

Eliason, M. J. "Accounts of Sexual Identity Formation in Heterosexual Students." *Sex Roles,* 1995, *32,* 821–834.

Evans, N. J. "The Impact of an LGBT Safe Zone Project on Campus Climate." *Journal of College Student Development,* 2002, *43,* 522–539.

Evans, N. J., and Herriott, T. K. "Freshman Impressions: How Investigating the Campus Climate for LGBT Students Affected Four Freshmen Students." *Journal of College Student Development,* 2004, *45,* 316–332.

Evans, N. J., and Wall, V. A. "Parting Thoughts: An Agenda for Addressing Sexual Orientation Issues on Campus." In V. A. Wall and N. J. Evans (eds.), *Toward Acceptance: Sexual Orientation Issues on Campus.* Lanham, Md.: American College Personnel Association, 2000.

Fassinger, R. E. "Lesbian, Gay, and Bisexual Identity and Student Development Theory." In R. L. Sanlo (ed.), *Working with Lesbian, Gay, Bisexual, and Transgender College Students: A Handbook for Faculty and Administrators.* Westport, Conn.: Greenwood Press, 1998.

Finkel, M. J., Storaasli, R. D., Bandele, A., and Schaefer, V. "Diversity Training in Graduate School: An Exploratory Evaluation of the Safe Zone Project." *Professional Psychology: Research and Practice,* 2003, *34,* 555–561.

Geasler, M. J., Croteau, J. M., Heineman, C. J., and Edlund, C. J. "A Qualitative Study of Students' Expression of Change After Attending a Panel Presentations by Lesbian, Gay, and Bisexual Speakers." *Journal of College Student Development,* 1995, *36,* 483–491.

Gelberg, S., and Chojnacki, J. T. "Developmental Transitions of Gay/Lesbian/Bisexual-Affirmative, Heterosexual Career Counselors." *Career Development Quarterly,* 1995, *43,* 267–273.

Grutzeck, S., and Gidycz, C. A. "The Effects of a Gay and Lesbian Speaker Panel on College Students' Attitudes and Behaviors: The Importance of Context Effects." *Imagination, Cognition and Personality,* 1997, *17*(1), 65–81.

Haddock, G., Zanna, M. P., and Esses, V. M. "Assessing the Structure of Prejudicial Attitudes: The Case of Attitudes Toward Homosexuals." *Journal of Personality and Social Psychology,* 1993, *65,* 1105–1118.

Hardiman, R., and Jackson, B. W. "Racial Identity Development: Understanding Racial Dynamics in College Classrooms and on Campus." In M. Adams (ed.), *Promoting Diversity in College Classrooms: Innovative Responses for the Curriculum, Faculty, and Institutions.* New Directions for Teaching and Learning, no. 52. San Francisco: Jossey-Bass, 1992.

Helms, J. E. "An Update of Helms' White and People of Color Identity Models." In J. G. Ponterotto, M. J. Casas, L. A. Suzuki, and C. M. Alexander (eds.), *Handbook of Multicultural Counseling.* Thousand Oaks, Calif.: Sage, 1995.

Herek, G. "The Social Psychology of Homophobia: Toward a Practical Theory." *Review of Law and Social Change,* 1986, *14*(4), 63–75.

Herek, G. "The Psychology of Sexual Prejudice." *Current Directions in Psychological Science,* 2000, *9*(1), 97–107.

Herek, G., and Capitanio, J. P. "'Some of My Best Friends': Intergroup Contact,

Concealable Stigma, and Heterosexuals' Attitudes Toward Gay Men and Lesbians." *Personality and Social Psychology Bulletin*, 1996, *22*, 412–424.

Hyde, J. S., and Jaffee, S. R. "Becoming a Heterosexual Adult: The Experiences of Young Women." *Journal of Social Issues*, 2000, *56*, 283–296.

Iasenza, S., and Troutt, B. V. "A Training Program to Diminish Prejudicial Attitudes in Student Leaders." *Journal of College Student Development*, 1990, *31*, 83–84.

Macintosh, M. "The Homosexual Role." In K. Plummer (ed.), *The Making of the Modern Homosexual*. Totowa, N.J.: Barnes and Noble Books, 1981. (Originally published 1968.)

Marcia, J. "Identity in Adolescence." In J. Adelson (ed.), *Handbook of Adolescent Psychology*. New York: Wiley, 1980.

Mohr, J. J. "Heterosexual Identity and the Heterosexual Therapist: An Identity Perspective on Sexual Orientation Dynamics in Psychotherapy." *Counseling Psychologist*, 2002, *30*, 532–566.

Nelson, E. S., and Krieger, S. L. "Changes in Attitudes Toward Homosexuality in College Students: Implementation of a Gay Men and Lesbian Peer Panel." *Journal of Homosexuality*, 1997, *33*(2), 63–81.

Oldham, J. D., and Kasser, T. "Attitude Change in Response to Information That Male Homosexuality Has a Biological Basis." *Journal of Sex and Marital Therapy*, 1999, *25*, 121–124.

Poynter, K. "What Is a Safe Zone? How Do I Find Information to Start a Heterosexual Ally Program on My Campus?" 2003. [http://www.lgbtcampus.org/faq/safe_zone.html].

Sax, L. J., and others. *The American Freshman: National Norms for Fall 2001*. Los Angeles: Higher Education Research Institute, University of California, Los Angeles, 2001.

Simoni, J. M., and Walters, K. L. "Heterosexual Identity and Heterosexism: Recognizing Privilege to Reduce Prejudice." *Journal of Homosexuality*, 2001, *41*(1), 157–172.

Sullivan, P. "Sexual Identity Development: The Importance of Target or Dominant Group Membership." In R. Sanlo (ed.), *Working with Lesbian, Gay, Bisexual, and Transgender College Students: A Handbook for Faculty and Administrators*. Westport, Conn.: Greenwood Press, 1998.

Washington, J., and Evans, N. J. "Becoming an Ally." In N. J. Evans and V. A. Wall (eds.), *Beyond Tolerance: Gays, Lesbians, and Bisexuals on Campus*. Alexandria, Va.: American College Personnel Association, 1991.

Waterman, A. D., Reid, J. D., Garfield, L. D., and Hoy, S. J. "From Curiosity to Care: Heterosexual Student Interest in Sexual Diversity Courses." *Teaching of Psychology*, 2001, *28*(1), 21–26.

Wilkinson, S., and Kitzinger, C. (eds.). *Heterosexuality: A Feminism and Psychology Reader*. Thousand Oaks, Calif.: Sage, 1993.

Worthington, R. L., Savoy, H. B., Dillon, F. R., and Vernaglia, E. R. "Heterosexual Identity Development: A Multidimensional Model of Individual and Social Identity." *Counseling Psychologist*, 2002, *30*, 496–531.

NANCY J. EVANS is professor and co-coordinator of the higher education program in the department of educational leadership and policy studies at Iowa State University.

ELLEN M. BROIDO is assistant professor of higher education and student affairs at Bowling Green State University in Ohio.

This chapter discusses the role of student affairs professionals in encouraging the development of racial justice allies through the exploration of whiteness.

Encouraging the Development of Racial Justice Allies

Robert D. Reason, Tara C. Scales,
Elizabeth A. Roosa Millar

If we believe, as Katz (2003) said, that "racism is a White problem" (p. 7), then we must also accept that white people have some responsibility to correct it. We start with the assumption that white people are both part of the cause and simultaneously victims of racism (Bower and Hunt, 1996). While people of color have been and continue to be the victims of egregious offenses at the hands of a few white Americans, racism and racial injustice insidiously enter into everyone's life by hindering the development of full and enriching relationships among people of different races. We therefore begin with the assumption that everyone would be better off if racism and racial injustice were eliminated.

Based on the definition of *social justice allies* on which this volume is built, the focus of this chapter is on white students and white student affairs professionals and their relationships with people of color. Given the context of power and privilege in the United States (McIntosh, 2001), whites continue to be members of the dominant social group who can choose to take action toward the elimination of racial injustice. When discussing issues of race and racism in the United States, it is often easy to think in terms of black and white. When reading this chapter, however, we encourage readers to be inclusive of all races.

The purpose of this chapter is to provide student affairs professionals with information and strategies necessary to become racial justice educators and encourage the development of racial justice ally attitudes and actions in the white students with whom they work. We present this chapter in three broad sections that we believe parallel the development of racial

NEW DIRECTIONS FOR STUDENT SERVICES, no. 110, Summer 2005 © Wiley Periodicals, Inc.

justice allies: (1) understanding racism, power, and privilege both intellectually and affectively; (2) developing a new white consciousness; and (3)
encouraging racial justice action.

We also believe that you cannot teach what you do not understand and
agree with Bishop (2002), who wrote, "If a person attempts ally education
who does not thoroughly grasp the concepts or demonstrate being an ally
in their own action . . . oppressive attitudes can be solidified and confirmed,
or backlash triggered. Those who suffer the most from this backfiring of
good intentions are those who are most vulnerable . . . because they are targets of oppression" (p. 128).

We therefore encourage all student affairs professionals to reflect on
their own racial justice attitudes and actions as they read this chapter. Student
affairs professionals must complete this process if they are to promote racial
justice ally development in the students they serve. In particular, white student affairs professionals who wish to develop their own racial justice attitudes and actions are encouraged to engage actively with the chapter.

We bring various perspectives to this chapter, including the voices of
dominant and target racial groups. The work we completed researching for
and writing this chapter has challenged each of us to explore more deeply
our racial identities and roles in racial justice movements. As an African
American woman, Tara understood the importance of developing racial
allies but approached our work through a different lens from Bob and
Liz—a lens she had not consciously used before. She was challenged by listening to the white students' struggle, recognizing that they were struggling
with her as a person of color, although she could not take their struggle
personally. Bob and Liz found themselves struggling through the process
that we write about: exploring their whiteness and ally identities. For Bob,
whiteness moved from an abstract concept to be studied to something
much more personal—something to be lived in his relationships. The process encouraged Liz to delve deeply into her multiple subjectivities, exploring for the first time how she made sense of the intersection between her
gender and race. The three of us emerge from this writing more deeply
grounded in our racial identities but left with the understanding that we
have a long way to go.

Understanding Racism and Privilege

Encouraging racial justice ally development starts with a thorough intellectual and affective understanding of racism and privilege. Recognizing
the structure of race in society, "wherein people are seen as part of larger
systems, shaped by context" (Bishop, 2002, p. 125), is an essential intellectual understanding. Recognizing one's own power and privilege, and its
impact on relationships with others, however, often leads to negative emotions like guilt or defensiveness that can become barriers to action if they
are not managed correctly (Johnson, 2000). Attending to the affective

component of this understanding thus becomes essential to the development of racial justice allies.

An Intellectual Understanding of Racism and Privilege. The literature related to racism and white allies reveals that intellectual understanding begins with a shared definition of key terms. Therefore, our first step provides a common language for discussion. We present structural, rather than individual, definitions of these emotionally charged concepts in order to encourage understanding among white students, while alleviating possible defensiveness and guilt which are barriers to a full understanding (Goodman, 2001; Johnson, 2000).

Racism. Racism is "any attitude, action, or institutional arrangement that results in the subordination of another group based ostensibly upon group-linked physical characteristics" (Jones, 2002, p. 30). Racism can manifest overtly or covertly, intentionally or unintentionally, individually or collectively.

Several types of racism exist: individual, institutional, and cultural (Jones, 2002). *Individual racism* "refers to the attitudes, behaviors, and beliefs of the individuals that result in unequal treatment of individuals on the basis of their racial or ethnic group" (p. 32); it can be intentional or unintentional. *Institutional racism* "is a pattern of racism embedded in the policies and practices of social institutions—the educational system, the legal system, the economic system, family, state, and religion—that has a negative impact upon certain ethnic groups" (p. 32). Institutional racism can also be intentional or unintentional and focuses on societal practices, not individual actions. Finally, *cultural racism* "refers to a devaluation of another racial or ethnic group's culturally different values and modes of behavior" (p. 32).

Contemporary Theories of Racism. Racism has evolved over the centuries from the widely held, and overtly accepted, notion of white supremacy to more covert forms (Ponterotto and Pedersen, 1993). Contemporary theories of racism emerged to address the seemingly contradictory values espoused by many whites, such as endorsing equal rights while rejecting governmental interventions meant to increase racial equity (Jones, 2002). These theories include symbolic racism and modern racism (whites believe that blacks violate the individualistic values and Protestant work ethic that guide white American ethos), ambivalent racism (whites have ambivalent feelings toward blacks resulting from two contradictory values—Protestant work ethic and egalitarianism), aversive racism (whites' racial views are internally inconsistent, causing conflict due to a belief in egalitarianism and negative feelings and beliefs toward blacks that are unacknowledged), and compunction theory (low-prejudiced whites experience compunction as a result of the discrepancy between their nonprejudiced personal beliefs and actual behaviors).

Although these theories were developed to describe racism by whites against blacks, social justice scholars recently have used these theories as effective lenses through which to understand white racism against other races. These theories, also called covert racism theories, offer an individual-level analysis of prejudice (Jones, 2002; Stephan and Stephan, 1996).

White Privilege. Perhaps the most widely recognized definition of white privilege is McIntosh's knapsack analogy (2001). McIntosh wrote that white privilege was "like an invisible weightless knapsack of special provisions, maps, passports, codebooks, visas, clothes, tools and blank checks" (p. 97) that whites are given at birth but people of color are denied.

The knapsack and its advantages are often unrecognized by those who possess it (Johnson, 2000; McIntosh, 2001). Johnson noted that the ability to remain unaware of privilege is a privilege in itself—what he called "epistemic privilege" (p. 24). Epistemic privilege allows whites to remain oblivious to these unearned assets and ignore the obstacles presented to people of color. Because they remain oblivious to assets and obstacles, epistemic privilege allows many whites to attribute their own success to "merit" while blaming people of color for not achieving at similar levels. Unrecognized privilege allows the "knapsack-haves" to blame the "knapsack-have-nots" without the discomfort of realizing their role in the problem.

A Word on the Importance of Language. We present these definitions to provide a common language and foundation on which to build. It is important that we as educators, and the students we hope to educate, possess a similar understanding and shared language to convey information. We must also recognize that each of the terms described above can be emotionally charged, accusatory, and painful (Johnson, 2000), especially for those who have not recognized their own privilege. Terms like *racism* and *privilege* can construct barriers, keeping otherwise good people from moving toward ally attitudes and actions.

Constructing this understanding as structural rather than personal is not meant to let white people off the hook of acknowledging their privilege. This strategy allows educators to start a conversation in a less-threatening manner until students are ready to address the affective components of racism and privilege, allowing them to come to know their students and plan effective racial justice interventions before resistance and defenses emerge (Adams, Jones, and Tatum, 1997). While understanding ultimately must move to a more personal, emotional level (Katz, 2003), this strategy allows the skilled facilitator to harness the emotions of the topic, to the benefit of students.

An Affective Understanding of Racism and Privilege. Once white students understand racism abstractly, they must learn how it affects them personally, a difficult and painful process (Bishop, 2002). Therefore, we now turn to a discussion of the emotions of racial justice ally development, especially the painful emotions arising early in the process as white students begin to recognize their own power and privilege. The painful emotions associated with the racial justice ally journey can either derail the process or motivate action, often depending on how racial justice educators recognize and manage them.

Recognizing the Emotions. Many racial justice educators cite fear and anxiety as the most prevalent emotions students experience (Goodman, 2001; Katz, 2003), likely resulting from the cognitive dissonance created by students' new understanding of power and privilege. These emotions, especially in white males, may be difficult to recognize as they manifest in resistance to racial justice education rather than more traditional expressions of fear or anxiety (Goodman, 2001).

Theories related to the ethical decision-making process, those decisions that require an individual to consider right and wrong, suggest that younger college students are likely to maintain an egocentric worldview that places consequences to them at the center of their decision-making process (Evans, Forney, and Guido-DiBrito, 1998). Emotional reactions and their resulting resistance based on perceived threats to the students' self-interests should be expected. Racial justice educators must find strategies that address these emotions at the egocentric level if they hope to counter these initial feelings effectively.

Managing the Emotions. Racial justice educators must move white students from the detached intellectual understanding of racism and privilege to a more personal affective understanding, all the while making certain that negative emotions do not derail the developmental process. Directing painful emotions to a positive end is not an easy task; a skilled educator must allow students to experience their own emotions but not allow the negative emotions to block action.

Goodman (2001) provides several strategies for managing the emotions evoked during racial justice training. Managing emotions can begin in the planning stage as long as racial justice educators provide clear expectations for their students. Students entering a new experience often seek structure. A lack of structure may exacerbate the cognitive dissonance at the root of many negative emotions. Providing guidelines for behavior during racial justice training activities may alleviate some cognitive dissonance, and thus negative emotional responses.

Acknowledging students' emotions, and the root of those emotions, is essential in managing them (Goodman, 2001). Providing a supportive environment for students to discuss, reflect on, and challenge emotions facilitates growth when done appropriately. Racial justice educators may consider anticipating common emotions before they arise in the group setting. Students may more readily acknowledge, work through, and move beyond negative emotions if they recognize them as a natural part of the developmental process.

Finally, racial justice educators must frame racial justice as beneficial to all races rather than a competition among them (Johnson, 2000). White students may initially feel threatened and defensive—needing to strike back—creating an inherent competition between whites and people of color. Although whites are asked to give up privilege in favor of racial justice, exploring racial justice as beneficial to all may assuage feelings rooted in a protection of self-interest.

Recognition and Development of a New White Consciousness

In a book written for white multicultural educators, Howard (1999) concluded a chapter on white racial identity by stating,

> Just as African Americans have challenged the negative associations of "Blackness" and chosen to recast their identity in their own positive image, so Whites need to acknowledge and work through the negative historical implications of "Whiteness" and create for ourselves a transformed identity as White people committed to equity and social change [p. 112].

We begin this section with Howard's goal in mind. We advocate for the new "positive white role model" identity that Tatum (2003) and others have challenged whites to find. We believe that in order to develop as allies, white people must develop an antiracist, privilege-cognizant white consciousness. Katz (2003) referred to developing this new sense of whiteness as "one of the most critical points" (p. 147) of a racial justice ally development process.

Student affairs professionals can assist students in the development of a positive white identity, just as we have historically assisted students in the development of other facets of identity. Several theories, models, and conceptualizations of whiteness have emerged in recent years. A familiarity with these ideas will assist student affairs professionals in encouraging students' racial development. It is also essential that student affairs professionals, whether white or persons of color, have a well-developed sense of their own racial identity.

Our Current Understanding of Whiteness. Most student affairs professionals, trained in student development theories, will recognize the role that race plays in creating an individual's understanding of their own identity. An appreciation for the social construction of identity (see Chapter One, this volume, for a complete discussion) encourages the exploration of the interaction of race with other personal characteristics for a complete understanding of how individuals make sense of their identities. That said, it is often easy to focus on the role of race in identity development for students of color and overlook its role in identity development for white students. We contend that white racial identity must be understood and attended to if the status quo is to be broken and movement toward a new white consciousness is to be made.

The first step toward a positive white racial identity, according to many early theories, is the recognition of "white" as a race and the abandonment of the racism inherent in society (Hardiman, 2001). Whites then move through a series of stages in which they confront previously unexamined assumptions about race (especially the superiority of whites), begin to try out a new and personal definition of whiteness based on new assumptions, and finally integrate fully a new, nonracist white identity. This process will be influenced greatly by the environment in which white students find themselves, the support (or resistance) they receive as they develop a racial identity, and the presence of a like-minded social group.

Although there are several other ways to conceptualize whiteness, for the purposes of ally development, understanding the process as one that moves from a naive, low-racial-salience position through an examination of whiteness to the development of a new, pro–racial justice understanding will suffice. It is important to note, however, that a strong connection exists between the process of white racial identity development and the process of cognitive and sociomoral development. The critical exploration of previously unexamined assumptions, and the ability to rectify successfully the dissonance that will be created in such an exploration, are higher-order cognitive skills. As King and Shuford (1996) noted, the "multicultural view" is a more cognitively complex view" (p. 153). Student affairs professionals therefore must maintain a developmental perspective, anticipating where students may be cognitively, as racial justice training programs are planned.

Developing a New Understanding of Whiteness. One essential strategy will be to encourage white students to reflect on their whiteness and the role that power and privilege play in their daily lives, especially in their relationships with people of color. Through reflection, students should come to understand the importance of being white in our society and the role whiteness plays in their relationships, both positive and negative. Reflection will likely evoke a new understanding of the racism that each of us holds, which can be a particularly painful revelation (Katz, 2003). At this point, students likely will equate whiteness with privilege (Tatum, 2003).

Impulsively translating the pain and guilt associated with the recognition of individual racism and unearned privilege into racial justice action often results in what Tatum (2003) called the "guilty White liberal persona" (p. 106); this action is intended to assuage guilt by proving to people of color that whites are overcoming their racism. Tatum suggested it may be beneficial for developing allies to identify recognized racial justice allies as a support network as they continue to redefine whiteness.

Just as there is no one way to understand Latino or African American identity, we do not have a single understanding of whiteness. That said, racial justice allies share several commonalties in their understanding of whiteness. First, whiteness is understood as having elements of a cultural heritage, but one distinct from privilege. Divorcing whiteness from a cultural heritage allows whites to hang on to a sense of color-blind individualism that obstructs racial justice ally development. Racial justice allies embrace a white culture (as they have defined it) but actively reject the power and privilege our society associates with being white. Embracing their whiteness means recognizing both the positive and negative attributes associated with it. A new understanding of whiteness requires an active "privilege-cognizant" (Bailey, 1998, p. 33) worldview at all times. Racial justice allies are critically aware of how and when privilege enters their daily lives.

For racial justice allies, a strong sense of whiteness must be accompanied by the moral courage to act differently from friends and family who may harbor feelings of racism (Stokes Brown, 2002). Taking a stand against racial injustice requires courage, fortitude, and confidence (Kivel, 2002). Bailey (1998) articulated the required courage more strongly when she encouraged readers to think of racial justice allies as "race traitors" (a moniker Bailey wears proudly) and likened this identity to "disembodied spectators and outsiders within" (p. 29). Whites who identify as racial justice allies therefore must be ready to live as outsiders within their own worlds.

A Caveat for White Student Affairs Professionals. We pause now to remind readers, specifically white readers, that we are discussing a process through which you must proceed if you wish to influence students. We remind you of Bishop's admonition (2002) that if one attempts to teach what is not personally understand, the situation will likely worsen. White student affairs professionals must continue to reflect on their own whiteness, their motivations for the racial justice actions they take, and the power and privilege that influence their lives. Redefining whiteness is not a process through which you lead students but one through which you travel *with* students.

Encouraging Racial Justice Action

Student affairs professionals who have provided the education and support for white students as they develop a new understanding of whiteness have already encouraged racial justice ally development. Ultimately, however, racial justice allies must take action to end the dominant racial ideology and culture that maintains social inequality (Goodman, 2001). White students with an understanding of racism and privilege, who have developed their own understanding of whiteness, may be ready to take action.

Following are several strategies to overcome resistance to racial justice education and move students to action. They are grounded in the discussion just presented as well as two extensive interview studies we conducted with students over the past years (Reason, Roosa Millar, and Scales, 2004). In one study, we interviewed upper-division white students who were recognized racial justice allies. In the other study, we interviewed three groups of first-year students: one group from a race relations course, one from an intentionally designed multicultural residence hall, and one with neither experience, drawn from a large introductory course. The intention of both studies was to begin to explicate relationships between college experiences and the development of racial justice allies. These students provided great insight into those experiences that encouraged, and those that impeded, their ally development:

• *Get to know your students around the issue* (Goodman, 2001). We assume that the development of racial justice allies is a process through which white students must travel. This assumption requires the acknowledgment that college students bring with them several years of previous experience. Effective education of all types begins by knowing the students, meeting them where they are, and nurturing their growth. Racial justice education is no different.

While some white students will arrive at college as emerging racial justice allies, many more will likely begin college naive about racial justice issues or with negative racial beliefs. Positive and negative messages received from family and secondary education shape the attitudes of entering college students (readers interested in the role of high schools in the development of racial justice allies are encouraged to read Perry, 2002). Student affairs professionals must engage students around the issue of racial justice in order to recognize and meet them where they are.

• *Educate students about white racial justice allies.* Tatum (2003) posited that a lack of positive white role models keeps whites from exploring the white racial consciousness needed for racial justice ally development. While we agree that identifying racial justice allies can be difficult, we also acknowledge a long history of white involvement in racial justice. Students need not start from scratch as they define their racial justice ally identity; they can build from those who have come before. Student affairs professionals can assist this process by educating students about the lives of historical and contemporary racial justice allies. We recommend books by Stokes Brown (2002) and O'Brien (2001), or exploration into the lives of Tim Wise, antiracist activist, author, and director of the newly formed Association for White Anti-Racist Education, and Morris Dees, noted civil rights attorney and cofounder of the Southern Poverty Law Clinic, as fine starting points for this education.

• *Help students make it personal.* In our studies, we found that younger students, who could not articulate how they were affected personally by racism or could not identify a friend who was negatively affected, were less likely to take racial justice actions. Recognizing this, student affairs professionals can assist white students to articulate where and how racism has negatively influenced their lives.

• *Encourage the development of empathy.* While some students will respond to egocentric motivations, others may respond more favorably to empathy. Encouraging students to talk with friends who have experienced racism may begin to build the "borrowed approximation" form of empathy (O'Brien, 2001), where white students vicariously experience the negative effects of racism. The short biographical writings in Terkel's work (1992) may also provide the connection to other college students' experiences needed to develop empathy. Student affairs professionals can encourage students involved in other social movements, or who may identify with other target groups, to explore how racial injustice is interrelated with other forms of injustice. This reflection builds on O'Brien's idea of "overlapping approximations."

• *Encourage students to "travel the world."* Bailey (1998) used the metaphor of "world travelers" for racial justice allies to reinforce the need for crossing racial borders in the pursuit of understanding. The metaphor also reinforces the amount of effort and discomfort needed to build and maintain a racial justice identity. Crossing borders requires one to actively remove oneself from a place of comfort and enter the unknown. Student affairs professionals can provide students both the challenge and support to "travel the world." Encouraging border crossing through the informal introduction of two students or formal programming may be effective means to this end. Greater connections with people of color, developed through this type of traveling, also will allow students to "borrow" approximations.

• *Invite students to take action.* Broido (2000), in her study of social justice allies, found that an invitation to action often was necessary for students to become involved. Student affairs professionals can, and should, invite interested students to explore and join racial justice groups, take a course on race relations, or enter into racial justice movements. Assisting students in identifying like-minded colleagues and building networks of racial justice allies also invites action.

• *Recognize and appreciate action at all levels.* We assume the racial justice ally development process is incremental and developmental. Therefore, student affairs professionals must recognize that students will be at different places within this process and have different comfort levels with their racial justice actions. As students redefine whiteness and their roles as outsiders-within, their comfort level with racial justice action should change. In our study, racial justice action took many forms on a continuum, from quiet and personal to highly visible group work. Young students discussed challenging friends on racist jokes and assumptions, while the recognized racial justice allies were involved with student government legislation, speaking out at rallies, and leading student groups. Student affairs professionals must recognize and celebrate all levels of racial justice action.

A Call to Action

So far, we have discussed the role of student affairs professionals in facilitating racial justice ally development in the students with whom they work. We turn now to, and close this chapter with, an equally important part of the racial justice ally development process: student affairs professionals as racial justice allies. Beyond facilitating student development, student affairs professionals must live as racial justice allies.

Student affairs professionals serve as role models for the college students with whom they work. One of the most effective ways to encourage the development of racial justice allies (and all social justice allies) may be for student affairs professionals to develop their own racial justice ally identities. All student affairs professionals should understand their own racial identity as well as the role power and privilege play in their relationships. They should be active, visible social justice advocates for all students (Evans and Reason, 2001, 2003) and role models of racial justice action. White student affairs professionals share a special responsibility to take action as racial justice allies and serve as positive white racial role models (Tatum, 2003). One cannot teach what one does not know (Bishop, 2002; Howard, 1999). If we hope to influence racial justice action positively, we must prove ourselves as racial justice allies.

References

Adams, M., Jones, J., and Tatum, B. D. "Knowing Our Students." In M. Adams, L. A. Bell, and P. Griffin (eds.), *Teaching for Diversity and Social Justice: A Sourcebook.* New York: Routledge, 1997.

Bailey, A. "Locating Traitorous Identities: Toward a View of Privilege-Cognizant White Character." *Hypatia*, 1998, *13*(3), 27–43.

Bishop, A. *Becoming an Ally: Breaking the Cycle of Oppression in People.* (2nd ed.) Halifax, Nova Scotia: Fernwood, 2002.

Bower, B. P., and Hunt, R. G. (eds.). *Impacts of Racism on White Americans.* (2nd ed.) Thousand Oaks, Calif.: Sage, 1996.

Broido, E. M. "The Development of Social Justice Allies During College: A Phenomenological Investigation." *Journal of College Student Development*, 2000, *41*, 3–18.

Evans, N. J., Forney, D. S., and Guido-DiBrito, F. *Student Development in College: Theory, Research, and Practice.* San Francisco: Jossey-Bass, 1998.

Evans, N. J., and Reason, R. D. "Guiding Principles: A Review and Analysis of Student Affairs Philosophical Statements." *Journal of College Student Development*, 2001, *42*, 359–377.

Evans, N. J., and Reason, R. D. "A Call to Advocacy and Activism." *ACPA Developments*, 2003, *30*(3), 5, 8. [http://www.myacpa.org/pub/documents/developmentsSept03_000.pdf].

Goodman, D. J. *Promoting Diversity and Social Justice: Educating People from Privileged Groups.* Thousand Oaks, Calif.: Sage, 2001.

Hardiman, R. "Reflections on White Racial Identity Development." In C. L. Wijeyesinghe and B. W. Jackson III (eds.), *New Perspectives on Racial Identity Development: A Theoretical and Practical Anthology.* New York: New York University Press, 2001.

Howard, G. R. *We Can't Teach What We Don't Know: White Teachers, Multiracial Schools.* New York: Teachers College Press, 1999.

Johnson, A. *Privilege, Power, and Difference.* New York: McGraw-Hill, 2000.

Jones, M. *Social Psychology of Prejudice.* Upper Saddle River, N.J.: Prentice Hall, 2002.

Katz, J. H. *White Awareness: Handbook for Anti-Racism Training.* (2nd ed.) Norman: University of Oklahoma Press, 2003.

King, P. M., and Shuford, B. C. "A Multicultural View Is a More Cognitively Complex View: Cognitive Development and Multicultural Education." *American Behavioral Scientist*, 1996, *40*, 153–164.

Kivel, P. *Uprooting Racism: How White People Can Work for Racial Justice.* (Rev. ed.) Gabriola Island, B.C., Canada: New Society Publishers, 2002.

McIntosh, P. "White Privilege and Male Privilege: A Personal Account of Coming to See Correspondences Through Work in Women's Studies." In M. L. Andersen and P. Hill Collins (eds.), *Race, Class, and Gender: An Anthology.* Belmont, Calif.: Wadsworth, 2001.

O'Brien, E. *Whites Confront Racism: Antiracists and Their Paths to Action.* Lanham, Md.: Rowman and Littlefield, 2001.

Perry, P. *Shades of White: White Kids and Racial Identities in High School.* Durham, N.C.: Duke University Press, 2002.

Ponterotto, J. G., and Pedersen, P. B. *Preventing Prejudice: A Guide for Counselors and Educators.* Thousand Oaks, Calif.: Sage, 1993.

Reason, R. D., Roosa Millar, E. A., and Scales, T. C. "Toward a Model of Interracial Social Justice Ally Development." Paper presented at the annual conference of the Association for the Study of Higher Education, Kansas City, Mo., Nov. 2004.

Stephan, W. G., and Stephan, C. W. *Intergroup Relations.* Boulder, Colo.: Westview Press, 1996.

Stokes Brown, C. *Refusing Racism: White Allies and the Struggle for Civil Rights.* New York: Teachers College Press, 2002.

Tatum, B. D. *"Why Are All the Black Kids Sitting Together in the Cafeteria?" and Other Conversations About Race.* New York: Basic Books, 2003.

Terkel, S. (ed.). *Race: How Blacks and Whites Think and Feel About the American Obsession.* New York: New Press, 1992.

ROBERT D. REASON is assistant professor of education and professor-in-charge of the college student affairs program at Penn State University. He is also a research associate in Penn State's Center for the Study of Higher Education.

TARA C. SCALES is a doctoral candidate in higher education and a graduate research assistant in the Center for the Study of Higher Education at Penn State University.

ELIZABETH A. ROOSA MILLAR is a doctoral candidate in higher education at Penn State University.

6

The authors advocate for a constructionist interpretation of disability, grounded in a social justice perspective, by discussing disability paradigms, factors that influence attitudes and attitude change regarding disability, and disability ally development and behaviors.

Encouraging the Development of Disability Allies

Nancy J. Evans, Jennifer L. Assadi, Todd K. Herriott

What does it mean to have a disability in today's society, and what does it mean to be a disability ally? As the literature we review on disability paradigms illustrates, the concept of disability has been given many meanings. While disability is usually considered an individual characteristic, social justice advocates, as well as others who come from a constructionist perspective, argue that it is society, not the individual, that creates disabilities by imposing standards of normalcy that exclude those who are different physically, emotionally, or cognitively. Disabled People's International (1982, as cited in Barnes and Mercer, 2003) made an important distinction between the concepts of impairment and disability, defining *impairment* as "the functional limitation within the individual caused by physical, mental, or sensory impairment" (p. 66) and *disability* as "the loss or limitation of opportunities to take part in the normal life of the community on an equal level with others due to physical and social barriers" (p. 66). Barnes and Mercer underscored that "the presence of an impairment does not mean automatic transfer to the status of a disabled person. It becomes an issue at the point where social barriers exclude that individual from participation in everyday activities" (p. 66). We subscribe to a constructionist philosophy while acknowledging that persons' unique selves, including their physical, emotional, and mental capacities, as well as their other social identities (for example, gender, ethnicity, and sexual orientation), greatly influence their worldview, self-perceptions, and how they are perceived and treated by others.

The concept of disability allies appears to be nonexistent in the literature. Our review suggests that while allies have been defined in a general sense, the idea of being an ally to persons with disabilities has previously gone unexplored, at least with regard to the scholarship of student affairs and related professions. Why is that? Recall the definition of social justice allies presented in Chapter One (this volume): "members of dominant social groups (e.g., men, Whites, heterosexuals) who are working to end the system of oppression that gives them greater privilege and power based upon their social group membership" (Broido, 2000, p. 3). We propose that the pervasive societal view of disability as an innate medical condition rather than a creation of societal oppression precludes an understanding that individuals with disabilities would benefit from or need allies. Changing this attitude and increasing awareness among individuals who are not disabled that their able-bodied identity is ascribed and affords them power and privilege is a necessary first step in developing disability allies.

In addition, most people, particularly college students, faculty, and staff, have had little contact with individuals with disabilities. Until the passage of Section 504 of the Rehabilitation Act of 1973 and the Americans with Disabilities Act of 1990, people with disabilities did not attend college in great numbers, and at the presecondary level, children with disabilities often attended separate schools (Hall and Belch, 2000). As a result, few people have had the opportunity to learn about various impairments and to understand the experiences of individuals with those impairments. Lack of interaction with individuals with disabilities can result in attitudes of superiority or panic, either of which may be the result of fear of appearing stupid or not knowing what to do (Marks, 1999).

In this chapter, we first review the paradigms through which disability has been understood and the implications of each. We then examine research on attitudes toward individuals with disabilities and ways to create attitude change and encourage ally development. Next, we present findings of a study we conducted that suggests ways in which individuals who are not disabled can be allies to students with disabilities. Finally, we discuss actions that disability allies can take to work for social justice.

We approach this topic with varied worldviews that have shaped our thinking. Nancy Evans is a person with mobility impairment caused by childhood polio. In recent years, she has experienced post-polio syndrome involving increasing weakness and fatigue, leading her to use a wheelchair most of the time. Only in the past few years has she begun a scholarly exploration of the topic of disability and its implications for college students as well as herself. Jennifer Assadi identifies as a disability ally. Prior to college, she had minimal contact with and knowledge of people with disabilities. She began to learn more by joining a research team that studied the out-of-class experiences of students with disabilities and working closely with Nancy. Through these experiences, she has become aware of the difficulties individuals with disabilities face daily and has become sensitive to their needs and challenges, which has encouraged her to educate herself and others further. Todd Herriott is also a disability ally and is an advocate working in higher education. As a student affairs professional who provides services to both students who identify as having a disability and institutional agents to ensure equal access as mandated by federal legislation, he has begun to critically examine the manner in which students with disabilities are served. Recently he has been exploring methods of changing institutional paradigms regarding disability services to ones that are grounded in a social constructivist perspective.

Disability Paradigms

The medical model has historically shaped society's view of disability (Hughes, 2002). As Hughes noted, "Disability has been understood as a sickness, and disabled people have been understood as invalids" (p. 58). Within this framework, the lives of persons with disabilities are assumed to center around their inability to do things and their need to be taken care of by others (Michalko, 2002).

A less pejorative, and therefore more acceptable, relabeling of the medical model, the *functional limitations approach* (Jones, 1996), focuses on the ways in which disability affects individuals' ability to perform everyday tasks within the parameters of what is considered "normal." Individuals using this perspective still view disability as "an individual matter requiring individual adaptation" (Michalko, 2002, p. 161). They ignore the fact that society normalizes being able-bodied as the accepted way of being (Michalko, 2002).

In reaction to the patronizing and debilitating manner in which individuals with disabilities have been treated in society, disability rights activists have called for the development of a collective disability identity that is political in nature and rejects society's view of impairment as an impediment (Michalko, 2002). This minority group paradigm emphasizes the common experiences of oppression, alienation, and discrimination that individuals with disabilities experience (Jones, 1996). Although this view of disability emphasizes group identity rather than individual identity, it still focuses on the victimization of individuals with disabilities and ways that individuals must address the injustices they face.

The social construction model of disability shifts attention from the individual to society. Adherents of this perspective argue that "impairment only becomes disabling because of social structures and organization" (Marks, 1999, p. 77). In effect, society creates disability by defining what is normal and what is abnormal or pathological rather than merely different. Fine and Asch (2000) noted that "by concentrating on cure or on psychological and physical restoration of the impaired person, society and the discipline of psychology have avoided the need to focus on essential changes in the environmental side of the 'person-in-environment' situation" (p. 338).

Combining elements of the minority group model and the social constructionist perspective,

> Disability oppression theory describes the pervasive and systematic nature of discrimination toward people with disabilities . . . [and] identifies the process by which people with disabilities journey toward empowerment and liberation through the establishment of equitable access to accommodation within society's systems, and through the creation of an interdependent social structure in which all persons are connected and depend on each other [Castañeda and Peters, 2000, p. 320].

This approach focuses on elimination of "ableism," defined by Rauscher and McClintock (1997) as "a pervasive system of discrimination and exclusion that oppresses people who have mental, emotional, and physical disabilities . . . [and] operates on individual, institutional, and societal/cultural levels" (p. 198). The goal of the disability oppression approach (also called the *social justice approach*) is to break down the rigid cultural norms that define what is normal so that physical, emotional, cognitive, and sensory differences are accepted and valued (Rauscher and McClintock, 1997). This approach also acknowledges the roles played by varying social identities in the experiences of people with impairments and takes into account differences in the perceptions and lived experiences of individuals based on context and the nature of their impairment (Castañeda and Peters, 2000).

Attitudes Toward Individuals with Disabilities

Encouraging and developing social justice attitudes and actions among students who are not disabled is necessary in order to help reduce the overt and covert barriers that exist for persons with disabilities and increase the number of disability allies in society. To accomplish this goal, there must be a clear understanding of the attitudes that exist toward individuals with disabilities and sound suggestions for transforming negative attitudes into positive ones.

Factors Influencing Disability Attitudes. Researchers have conducted hundreds of studies examining individuals' attitudes toward people with disabilities in a variety of settings, such as employment, education, and the human services field. Favazza, Kumar, and Phillipsen (as cited in Baer, Hammond, and Warren, 2004) suggested that attitudes toward individuals with disabilities are formed by three major factors: indirect experiences (how individuals with disabilities are portrayed in books, movies, and other media), direct experiences, and the attitudes of one's primary social group (such as parents and peers) toward persons with disabilities. Other influential factors are contact, information, and communication.

Contact. Researchers have paid significant attention to ways that contact can influence an individual's attitude toward disability. Hannah (1988) suggested that positive attitudes could be the result of pleasant interactions, whereas negative attitudes could be caused by an unpleasant interaction. Several researchers reported that positive attitudes were developed when structured contact was created between students with disabilities and those without disabilities (Brownlee and Carrington, 2000; Maras and Brown, 1996; Slininger, Sherrill, and Jankowski, 2000).

Berry and Jones (1991) found that students who were not disabled developed negative attitudes toward students with disabilities when they experienced little control over the contact and the contact was perceived as more intimate. Similarly, Fichten (1988) found that social distance, a term she used to refer to both proximity and length of interaction, affected disability attitudes of college students. For example, for relatively distant situations, such as being in a large lecture class with a student with a disability, where the likelihood of extensive interaction is minimal, attitudes were generally favorable; however, for closer situations, such as being assigned a roommate with a disability, attitudes tended to be more negative. The amount of contact has also been found to affect attitudes in a positive manner. Students who are able-bodied who experienced a high level of contact with students who have impairments showed significant gains in their level of acceptance (Favazza and Odom, 1997). In addition, Yuker (1994) reported that "there are positive attitudes when contact with disabled people includes equal status, cooperative interdependence, support from authority figures, and opportunities for individualizing outgroup members" (p. 7).

Information. Knowledge or information has been found to have an impact on the attitudes that students who are not disabled develop toward students with impairments (Yuker, 1994). Knowledge can increase one's level of perceived competence in interacting with individuals with disabilities, which researchers have found creates more favorable attitudes toward persons with disabilities (Kowalski and Rizzo, 1996). Exposing students to a curriculum that teaches about disabilities increases their awareness and knowledge and leads to more positive attitudes toward individuals with disabilities, but the literature used must be accurate and followed by a structured discussion (Andrews, 1998; Baer, Hammond, and Warren, 2004; Campbell, Gilmore, and Cuskelly, 2003).

Kelly, Sedlacek, and Scales (1994) found that college students who are not disabled form opinions regarding students with disabilities in stereotypical manners. By increasing knowledge, students who are not disabled may learn ways in which they are similar to students with disabilities, thus reducing the extent of negative attitudes held toward individuals with disabilities. In addition, this increase in knowledge may reduce the amount of stereotypical bias that students who are not disabled hold about students with disabilities.

Communication. Researchers have found that communication and language affect attitudes toward persons with disabilities. Makas (1988) found that persons with disabilities and those without disabilities differ significantly in what they perceive as being positive attitudes toward persons with disabilities. For example, the perfectly good intention of a person who is not disabled could be perceived as negative (degrading) by a person with a disability, thus causing that person to respond negatively. Tregaskis (2000) suggested that to encourage positive attitudes, a common language related to concepts such as impairment, disability, and exclusion needs to be shared between persons with disabilities and those without disabilities.

Disability Attitude Change. Similar to most salient attitudes, those toward people with disabilities are difficult to change, and according to Horne (1988), research has yet to identify a specific procedure that is always effective in producing positive change. However, role-plays and simulations and a combination of contact and information have encouraged attitude change.

Role-Plays and Simulations. Fichten (1988) suggested that role-plays that are structured as problem-solving exercises may encourage more positive attitudes. Wesson and Mandell (1989) noted that simulation activities (such as walking blindfolded, trying to read braille, or using a wheelchair) can be successful in improving the attitudes of students who are not disabled toward those who are. This is particularly the case if the activity appears to be a real experience that the individual will take seriously, is repeated a minimum of four times so the participant has repeated chances to determine how the task can be accomplished, and is observed by a peer, parent, sibling, or roommate since research has demonstrated that people are more engaged in activities if they are observed. In addition, participants should be given clear instructions so the activities are understood and done correctly, and they should reflect on the experience through writing or discussion, since reflection contributes to internalization of experiences.

Combining Contact and Information. Many researchers have found that to change attitudes, contact and knowledge must be combined (Pernice and Lys, 1996; Fichten, 1988; Horne, 1988). Beattie, Anderson, and Antonak (1997) reported that a more favorable attitude toward students with disabilities can be developed by combining information, indirect contact (such as viewing videotapes), and direct contact (for example, having a professor with a visible disability). Yuker (1994) suggested that an attitudinal shift may occur if the following conditions exist between students with disabilities and those without disabilities: equal status, common goals, intimate rather than casual contact, and a pleasant or rewarding contact.

Encouraging Disability Ally Development

Developing positive attitudes toward individuals with disabilities is a necessary but not sufficient first step in becoming a disability ally. Additional learning is needed to support individuals with disabilities and advocate for social justice for this population. There has been a paucity of scholarship addressing strategies for encouraging the development of disability allies. Therefore, the following suggestions are based on literature about ally development in general and ally development for other groups (for example, women, persons of color, and lesbian, gay, bisexual, and transgender individuals). We are careful to note some of the unique challenges that face disability allies.

Washington and Evans (1991) cite awareness as the first level of ally development. From a social justice perspective, awareness of an issue provides opportunity to examine it critically and determine strategies for change. People rarely speak about disability, and the information that is available is often stereotypical and misleading. As a result, individuals who are not disabled know very little about the causes and ramifications of disability. Increasing the visibility of disability issues and individuals with disabilities is important on college campuses to create awareness and encourage persons who are not disabled to become disability allies.

Awareness of an issue must be followed with education (Washington and Evans, 1991). Successful disability-related changes are most likely to occur when people are educated about the issues (Caras, 2004). Accurate information is necessary to dismantle the self-perpetuating cycle of oppression that feeds on each successive generation's simply accepting the norms and cultural understanding of the previous generation. Incorporating education about disabilities into course work and programming, ensuring that libraries have books and other media about disability, and encouraging students to interact with persons with disabilities are critical factors in ally development. Helpful educational resources include Marks (1999), Barnes and Mercer (2003), and Linton (1998). In addition, the Web sites of the Association on Higher Education and Disability (http://www.ahead.org/), the HEATH Resource Center at George Washington University (http://www.heath.gwu.edu/index.html), and the Standing Committee on Disability of the American College Personnel Association (http://www.myacpa.org/sc/cd/) provide up-to-date information about disability issues in higher education.

The third level of ally development is the development of skills (Washington and Evans, 1991). Necessary skills include communication strategies to counter oppression, such as open and honest dialogue between individuals with disabilities and those without disabilities (Brownlee and Carrington, 2000); organizational techniques to facilitate change, such as Creamer and Creamer's model of planned change (1986); and critical thinking that challenges and dismantles barriers on both a micro and macro level. Skills can be taught in structured ally development programs or social justice classes, or through mentoring.

Ally Behaviors and Actions

Once individuals move through the first three levels of ally development, they have the ability to put their learning into practice through action (Washington and Evans, 1991). In the following two sections, we discuss ways in which allies can help to create a just campus environment for students with disabilities. First, we present the suggestions of several students with impairments with whom we spoke during a study of involvement. Then we consider specific strategies based on social justice principles.

Suggestions from Students with Impairments. The authors of this chapter, collaborating with two other researchers (Evans and others, 2004), conducted a phenomenological study to explore the out-of-class experiences of students with impairments. We divided the students into five groups based on impairment similarities. Each researcher interviewed two respondents and conducted a focus group with students in one of these groups. Through conducting this research, we identified ways in which students with disabilities thought students without disabilities could be supportive.

The first suggestion was for students who do not have disabilities to be encouraging and helpful in their interactions with students with disabilities. Jessica (all names used are pseudonyms) was diagnosed with muscular dystrophy and has had significant loss of fine motor skills and muscle strength in her extremities; she uses an electric wheelchair. She recalled how women without disabilities "drug" her along to different events, thereby encouraging her to be involved:

> I was in choir in high school and somebody on my dorm floor said that they're having try-outs . . . for [college] choir. . . . , so I went . . . , her just kinda dragging me along. . . . This [other] girl I know who's in one of my classes. . . . she drug me to this off-campus meeting. . . . It's . . . a social gathering . . . and that's where I met [the friends with whom I now socialize].

Courtney, another student with mobility impairment, expressed similar feelings. She was in a farm accident at a young age that paralyzed her from the waist down so she uses a manual wheelchair. She talked about how other students in band helped her get up the ramp and through doors, which resulted in her feeling like "a part of the group." While Jessica and Courtney stressed that students without disabilities can be supportive by being encouraging and helpful, one must keep in mind not to overdo it. Respecting the autonomy of individuals is important as well. An attitude that suggests that one knows what is best for an individual with a disability is condescending and insensitive.

The second way in which these students thought students without disabilities could be supportive was by increasing their awareness and learning more accurate information about disabilities. One way to learn more is by asking questions. Kay, a twenty-one-year-old junior, was diagnosed with a hearing impairment at the age of two. She shared her feelings about students who did not have disabilities asking her about what it is like to be deaf: "Well, if they REALLY want to learn from me, then that's great. I like it when they ask me and . . . they obviously want to know more. . . . I think that's really cool and I feel like I have a kinship with those kinds of people."

When students who do not have disabilities are not aware and do not appear to be interested in learning more, it can be a disheartening experience.

Jamal, a student diagnosed with depression and social anxiety disorder, shared his frustrations with the lack of understanding of mental illness:

> [Other students] don't want to hear about it. You know, if somebody has cancer, they are going to talk about it. But, if somebody has depression, it's just, "Oh, everybody gets down sometimes." If somebody has generalized anxiety, then it's, "Oh, everybody has stress, just deal with it.". . . You don't see [any awareness campaigns for mental illness]. What you do see is the little Zoloft guy bouncing around on commercials saying, "Oh, do you feel blue?"

Jamal's comments reveal the ignorance that individuals can exhibit about mental illness and the inaccurate information that the general public receives from the media. Students who want to be disability allies must learn to distinguish what is reality and what is not by educating themselves about various impairments and the inaccurate ways in which the media often portray them.

Finally, one student diagnosed with attention deficit–hyperactivity disorder talked about how students who are not disabled need to increase their knowledge so they would know that students with disabilities are not "breakable." James, a member of a fraternity, reported, "The president and the chaplain don't want me to be involved in the house very much anymore because they don't feel like I can mentally handle it, which isn't really true, but that's just their stigma." James's comments reveal how a lack of knowledge can cause fear. Any student who wishes to be a disability ally must take steps to learn accurate information in order to dispel the myths and fears that exist about persons with disabilities.

Ways of Being a Disability Ally. Given societal attitudes toward individuals with disabilities, we caution readers to carefully consider their motivations for working with this population. Too often individuals become "pseudo-allies" for one of three reasons: (1) to make themselves look good, (2) to benefit from providing services to those with disabilities, or (3) to "help the less fortunate" (Annette, n.d.). In the first case, pseudo-allies take advantage of individuals with disabilities for their personal benefit; in the second, they exploit individuals with disabilities; and in the third, they treat individuals with disabilities in a patronizing and condescending manner. To be true disability allies, individuals must work with persons with disabilities, seeing and treating them as equals deserving of respect.

The following are actions that allies can take to work effectively with persons with disabilities. These strategies focus on self-education, awareness raising and advocacy, and direct action. Many of the strategies we suggest draw on concepts associated with Universal Design, defined by the Center for Universal Design at North Carolina State University (1997) as "the design of products and environments to be usable by all people to the greatest extent possible, without the need for adaptation or specialized design" (p. 1). Essential to this idea is the notion that inclusion rather than adaptation or accommodation should be the goal.

Self-Education. Educating oneself is an ongoing process. We encourage allies to learn everything they can about the oppression of persons with disabilities through reading, asking questions, and listening to others. Allies must always be aware of their own privilege as persons who are not disabled and must be open to having others point out when their own behaviors exhibit oppression. Viewing situations and environments from the perspective of a person with a disability is another important learning strategy. We encourage allies to imagine what their experience might be like if they had specific access issues and to listen to the expressed needs and experiences of those who identify as having an impairment.

Awareness Raising and Advocacy. A major role that allies can play is questioning accepted practice in order to raise awareness of ways in which individuals with disabilities are oppressed. Questioning involves critically examining the assumptions and expectations of society about how things are done. Examples of awareness-raising behaviors include:

- Asking about the availability of alternative formats when handouts or other materials are distributed and requesting that the issue be addressed if none are available
- When attending events, noticing if the location is accessible from both a physical and communication perspective and inquiring with event sponsors or organizers about access issues
- Questioning behavior or words that continue the pattern of oppression toward persons with disabilities
- Talking with members of social identity groups with whom one identifies about issues of disability oppression to help them understand the links among different forms of oppression
- Working to ensure that disability issues are included when diversity is addressed in schools and in the workplace
- Working to counter discrimination in housing, employment, and membership or participation in organizations and activities

Direct Action. It is not sufficient to cognitively agree with the concept of social justice as it applies to persons with disabilities or even to advocate on behalf of this population; true allies live their lives in accordance with their beliefs. Direct actions that allies can take include:

- Supporting persons with disabilities in taking leadership roles.
- Proactively addressing access issues rather than leaving it up to members of the oppressed group to take action (for example, not patronizing places that are inaccessible).
- Making one's home or environment accessible to persons with disabilities.

- Countering, on a person-to-person level, stereotypes, misconceptions, and conventional wisdom about the nature of disability and about how people with disabilities perceive, think, feel, act, and comprehend.
- Challenging and intervening to prevent harassment, bullying, and other forms of overt hostility.
- Providing solidarity in numbers through ally-to-ally outreach.
- Being a "safe person" for persons in the process of disclosure of disability status. The parallels between coming out for lesbian, gay, bisexual, and transgender people and disclosure for people with nonapparent disabilities are particularly striking.
- Raising one's children with disabilities to be effective self-advocates.
- Raising one's children who are not disabled to be effective allies.

Conclusion

Social change is created through thoughts, words, and actions. Student affairs professionals have an obligation to educate themselves so they have accurate information about disability and the experiences of students who are disabled. They must also serve as advocates for disability awareness and changes in policy and practice to ensure that individuals with impairments are treated equitably on college campuses. Finally, they have a responsibility to take action when oppression occurs and to work alongside individuals with disabilities to create a positive learning environment in which all students can succeed. If student affairs professionals model these behaviors, students will learn from their example, and disability allies will become a reality on college campuses rather than just a good idea proposed in this volume.

References

Andrews, S. E. "Using Inclusion Literature to Promote Positive Attitudes Toward Disabilities." *Journal of Adolescent and Adult Literacy*, 1998, *41*, 420–427.

Annette, A. "On the Question of Allies." N.d. [http:www.madknight.com/pep/allies.htm].

Baer, R. D., Hammond, M., and Warren, C. "Educating Youth About Disabilities and Disabilities Careers: Preliminary Field Test Results." *Center for Persons with Disabilities News*, 2004, *27*(2), 1–7. [http://www.cpd.usu.edu/newsletters/PDF/ CPDNews v27No2.pdf].

Barnes, C., and Mercer, G. *Disability: Key Concepts*. Cambridge: Polity, 2003.

Beattie, J. R., Anderson, R. J., and Antonak, R. F. "Modifying Attitudes of Prospective Educators Toward Students with Disabilities and Their Integration into Regular Classrooms." *Journal of Psychology*, 1997, *13*, 245–259.

Berry, J. G., and Jones, W. H. "Situational and Dispositional Components of Reaction Toward Persons with Disabilities." *Journal of Social Psychology*, 1991, *131*, 673–684.

Broido, E. M. "The Development of Social Justice Allies During College: A Phenomenological Investigation." *Journal of College Student Development*, 2000, *41*, 3–18.

Brownlee, J., and Carrington, S. "Opportunities for Authentic Experience and Reflection: A Teaching Programme Designed to Change Attitudes Towards Disability for Pre-Service Teachers." *Support for Learning*, 2000, *15*(3), 99–105.

Campbell, J., Gilmore, L., and Cuskelly, M. "Changing Student Teachers Attitudes Towards Disability and Inclusion." *Journal of Intellectual and Developmental Disability,* 2003, *28,* 369–380.

Caras, S. "Summit on Human Rights and Disability." 2004. [http://www.peoplewho. net/documents/convention.htm].

Castañeda, R., and Peters, M. L. "Ableism." In M. Adams and others (eds.), *Readings for Diversity and Social Justice.* New York: Routledge, 2000.

Center for Universal Design. *The Principles of Universal Design.* (Version 2.0) Raleigh: North Carolina State University, 1997.

Creamer, D. G., and Creamer, E. G. "Applying a Model of Planned Change to Program Innovation in Student Affairs." *Journal of College Student Personnel,* 1986, *27,* 431–437.

Evans, N. J., and others. [Social integration of students with disabilities]. Unpublished raw data, 2004.

Favazza, P. C., and Odom, S. L. "Promoting Positive Attitudes of Kindergarten-Age Children Toward People with Disabilities." *Exceptional Children,* 1997, *63,* 405–418.

Fichten, C. S. "Students with Physical Disabilities in Higher Education: Attitudes and Beliefs That Affect Integration." In H. E. Yuker (ed.), *Attitudes Toward Persons with Disabilities.* New York: Springer, 1988.

Fine, M., and Asch, A. "Disability Beyond Stigma: Social Interaction, Discrimination, and Activism." In M. Adams and others (eds.), *Readings for Diversity and Social Justice.* New York: Routledge, 2000.

Hall, L. M., and Belch, H. A. "Setting the Context: Reconsidering the Principles of Full Participation and Meaningful Access for Students with Disabilities." In H. A. Belch (ed.), *Serving Students with Disabilities.* New Directions for Student Services, no. 91. San Francisco: Jossey-Bass, 2000.

Hannah, M. E. "Teacher Attitudes Toward Children with Disabilities: An Ecological Analysis." In H. E. Yuker (ed.), *Attitudes Toward Persons with Disabilities.* New York: Springer, 1988.

Horne, M. D. "Modifying Peer Attitudes Toward the Handicapped: Procedures and Research Issues." In H. E. Yuker (ed.), *Attitudes Toward Persons with Disabilities.* New York: Springer, 1988.

Hughes, B. "Disability and the Body." In C. Barnes, M. Oliver, and L. Barton (eds.), *Disability Studies Today.* Cambridge: Polity, 2002.

Jones, S. R. "Toward Inclusive Theory: Disability as a Social Construction." *NASPA Journal,* 1996, *33,* 347–354.

Kelly, A. E., Sedlacek, W. E., and Scales, W. R. "How College Students with and Without Disabilities Perceive Themselves and Each Other." *Journal of Counseling and Development,* 1994, *73,* 178–182.

Kowalski, E., and Rizzo, T. "Factors Influencing Preservice Student Attitudes Toward Individuals with Disabilities." *Adapted Physical Activity Quarterly,* 1996, *13*(2), 180–196.

Linton, S. *Claiming Disability: Knowledge and Identity.* New York: New York University Press, 1998.

Makas, E. "Positive Attitudes Toward Disabled People: Disabled and Non-Disabled Persons' Perspective." *Journal of Social Issues,* 1988, *44,* 49–61.

Maras, P., and Brown, R. "Effects of Contact on Children's Attitudes Toward Disability." *Journal of Applied Social Psychology,* 1996, *26,* 2113–2134.

Marks, D. *Disability: Controversial Debates and Psychosocial Perspectives.* New York: Routledge, 1999.

Michalko, R. *The Difference That Disability Makes.* Philadelphia: Temple University Press, 2002.

Pernice, R., and Lys, K. "Interventions for Attitude Change Towards People with Disabilities: How Successful Are They?" *International Journal of Rehabilitation Research,* 1996, *19*(2), 171–174.

Rauscher, L., and McClintock, M. "Ableism Curriculum Design." In M. Adams, L. A. Bell, and P. Griffin (eds.), *Teaching for Diversity and Social Justice: A Sourcebook.* New York: Routledge, 1997.

Slininger, D., Sherrill, C., and Jankowski, C. M. "Children's Attitudes Toward Peers with Severe Disabilities: Revisiting Contact Theory." *Adapted Physical Activity Quarterly,* 2000, *17,* 176–196.

Tregaskis, C. "Interviewing Non-Disabled People About Their Disability-Related Attitudes: Seeking Methodologies." *Disability and Society,* 2000, *15,* 343–353.

Washington, J., and Evans, N. J. "Becoming an Ally." In N. J. Evans and V. A. Wall (eds.), *Beyond Tolerance: Gays, Lesbians and Bisexuals on Campus.* Washington, D.C.: American College Personnel Association, 1991.

Wesson, C., and Mandell, C. "Simulations: Promoting Understanding of Handicapping Conditions." *Teaching Exceptional Children,* 1989, 22(1), 32–35.

Yuker, H. E. "The Effects of Contact on Attitudes Toward Disabled Persons: Some Empirical Generalizations." In H. E. Yuker (ed.), *Attitudes Toward Persons with Disabilities.* New York: Springer, 1988.

NANCY J. EVANS *is professor and higher education program co-coordinator in the department of educational leadership and policy studies at Iowa State University.*

JENNIFER L. ASSADI *is a graduate student in higher education at Iowa State University.*

TODD K. HERRIOTT *is the Americans with Disabilities Act compliance officer and coordinator of disability services at Simmons College in Boston.*

This chapter discusses the difficulties associated with developing a social justice ally identity and provides practical suggestions to overcome them.

Issues and Strategies for Social Justice Allies (and the Student Affairs Professionals Who Hope to Encourage Them)

Robert D. Reason, Ellen M. Broido

As we sat down to draft this chapter, we struggled to determine its focus. Should we focus on ways that student affairs professionals and our students might act as allies, or should we focus on strategies that student affairs professionals might employ to best foster the development of allies? They are, of course, issues with considerable overlap. If ally work can be conceptualized, as Ellen has done previously (Broido, 2000b), as possessing three components (inspiring and educating dominant group members, creating institutional and cultural change, and supporting target group members), then developing the next generation of allies is indeed a key constituent of ally work.

We also spent considerable time discussing where self-understanding fits into this three-component model. A great deal of progress on social justice issues has come from people with limited self-understanding: dominant group members who lack self-awareness have been responsible for much social good. Self-understanding thus is not a prerequisite for ally action. However, we believe that effective and sustainable ally behavior requires a solid foundation of self-understanding—that is, understanding based on continuous critical reflection into the roles of power and privilege in one's life and relationships.

We begin this chapter with a discussion of self-understanding. We then explore each of the three components of ally work, including strategies to further each component. Rather than an exhaustive how-to list, however,

NEW DIRECTIONS FOR STUDENT SERVICES, no. 110, Summer 2005 © Wiley Periodicals, Inc.

we hope the strategies we present start a conversation that readers continue based on their circumstances and contexts. Finally, we highlight several obstacles and difficulties associated with being a social justice ally. Throughout this volume, we have maintained that a social justice ally identity is a difficult identity; this chapter explores some of those difficulties. We offer this final chapter as our best judgment, and the judgment of many of the authors from whom we have learned, how to overcome those difficulties and be effective social justice allies.

Self-Understanding

A critical understanding of one's role as a member of one or more dominant groups is not required for social justice ally action. Self-understanding, however, does provide the foundation on which sustainable ally identity and actions are built. Maintaining the motivation to act in the light of the difficulties that social justice allies face requires a degree of confidence and clarity of purpose that comes through critical reflection and a sense of moral imperative, both of which arise through understanding (Bishop, 2002). Ellen's own work (Broido, 2000a) reinforces the relationship between understanding of self, confidence in one's attitudes and abilities, and social justice actions. Recall also Howard's admonition (1999) that "you can't teach what you don't know." Teaching others about power, privilege, oppression, and the actions to counteract them requires a thorough understanding of the role these constructs play in one's own daily life.

We offer the following list of possible strategies as ways to enhance the critical self-awareness we are describing. We also see justice-cognizant identity as the goal of this process. A justice-cognizant identity, similar to but broader than Bailey's concept (1998) of the privilege-cognizant identity, requires a critical awareness of how one's behaviors, attitudes, actions, and lack of actions support justice for everyone. A constant awareness of one's position-related dominant and target group membership, a sensitivity to the effect of those positions on daily interactions, and recognition of the impact of one's actions are required of a justice-cognizant ally identity:

- Continue to read about and study issues of social justice, building an intellectual understanding of power, privilege, and oppression.
- Identify the multiple identities you possess, recognizing their interaction, the ways in which those identities may shift over your lifetime, and how their meaning may shift depending on context.
- Critically examine the role of your power, privilege, and oppression in your daily life, moving these three abstractions into concrete understandings.
- Avoid impulsive actions in favor of actions based in reflection, contemplation, and compassion, avoiding the "guilty liberal" impulse to action (Dass and Gorman, 1985; Tatum, 2003).

- Take time to struggle through the inevitable cognitive and affective dissonance created when good people recognize the realities of living within societal structures that reinforce inequality.
- Recognize and weigh the consequences (positive and negative) you may encounter in assuming a social justice ally identity. Are the possible positive outcomes worth the difficulties you may face?
- Be able to articulate why you do this work. What motivates you? How does this work fit with your own values, spiritual beliefs, and life purposes?
- Identify your own benefit in doing this work. Having a clear understanding of how your life would be better in the absence of oppression will help you withstand challenges to the work. Bowser and Hunt's *The Impacts of Racism on White Americans* (1996), while specific to racism, is an excellent resource on this topic.
- Know your own strengths and limits. Some of us are gifted teachers but less comfortable in more politicized situations. Some of us excel at organizing large groups of people; some of us can communicate in ways that are heard well by those with formal power. Few of us are equally effective in all arenas; knowing our talents will maximize our ability to create social change.

Ally Actions

Ally work can be conceptualized as three concurrent processes. Ellen (Broido, 2000b) originally developed this framework speaking to lesbian, gay, and bisexual allies, but it is easily expanded to all areas of social justice ally action (MacKinnon, Broido, and Wilson, 2004). There is, of course, considerable overlap in these areas. For example, allies can provide support to target members through their work in advocating for change in institutional policies. Nevertheless, it is useful to delineate these components separately in order to address each more fully.

Inspiring and Educating Dominant Group Members. One critical component of ally work is working with members of dominant social groups. That work can take many forms, but the most obvious of these is educating dominant group members about issues of social justice. Kivel (2002) reminds us that most people do not want to be agents of oppression, but that they lack the awareness that they are being oppressive, or information about how to act differently. Gaining information was a critical aspect of students' development as allies in Ellen's study (Broido, 2000a; see Chapter Two, this volume, for a more comprehensive discussion of types of information). Dass and Gorman (1985) highlighted the power of providing information when they wrote, "Sometimes it's enough just to share information with others. . . . We trust these situations to speak for themselves. Injustice will strike others as injustice has struck us. We're appealing to collective understanding and compassion" (p. 187).

Dass and Gorman (1985) also raise an important caution to our work as educators: they warn against using information to reinscribe our own power, to coerce rather than build collective consciousness and shared engagement:

> But much of the time we come into social action . . . and we're just a little self-righteous. We're convinced we've got something to say, something we're "correct" about. We've got our ideology and our scenario: here's how the situation really is, and the facts to back it up. . . . But at some level what we're communicating is the feeling that *we know*, others don't, and we've got to Change Minds. . . . There's often an air of superiority in what we say. People instinctively back off. They feel like they're being told, being "should" upon. Social action, they understand intuitively, ought to be fully voluntary if it's to have power and endurance [pp. 157–158].

In addition to educating dominant group members, another critical component is drawing allies into action by inspiring them, recruiting them, and making such actions expected. Allies in Ellen's study (Broido, 2000a) were drawn into social justice advocacy when they were expected to because of roles they held, or when they were invited into the work by others. Similar findings emerged from research Bob has completed (Reason, Roosa Millar, and Scales, 2004). Many students are reluctant to take action without encouragement and invitation, and student affairs professionals often are in positions to make such invitations. Our suggestions for inspiring, educating, and engaging dominant group members include the following:

- Engage with dominant group members in discussions about power, privilege, and oppressions of all types, even when such discussion may make others less comfortable. Incorporate those discussions into all facets of your work; social justice issues arise as much in talking about budget priorities as in programs focused specifically on oppression.
- Recognize and point out instances of power and privilege differentials during interactions with others. Do so to raise awareness.
- Study the history of social justice movements and the roles of dominant group members in those histories (Kivel, 2002). Talk with other dominant group members about what you learn. Challenge the myth that dominant group members cannot effect change.
- Confront inappropriate comments and behaviors in ways that educate rather than demean or embarrass.
- Develop confrontation skills that alleviate defensive reactions from other dominant group members. Johnson's book (2000) is a wonderful resource to assist in this endeavor.
- Create environments where ally behavior is expected. Incorporate expectations of ally behavior into guidelines for resident assistants, peer educators, orientation leaders, and other student leadership roles. Explicitly

invite students into ally behavior by asking them to join you and other student in ally actions.

- Persevere. Overcome initial defensiveness of dominant group members through prolonged engagement.

Creating Institutional and Cultural Change. Although everyone has a responsibility to challenge unjust policies, student affairs professionals, especially those in upper levels of the administration, have some level of influence that students do not share (although we often underestimate the power of an organized group of students to influence campus politics). These student affairs professionals share a responsibility to influence change on their campuses (Evans and Reason, 2001)—not only to intervene at the individual student level, but also to create environments in which all students, including social justice allies, can flourish. We offer the following suggestions for institution-level action:

- Support the recruitment and retention of diverse students, faculty, and staff. While most researchers have concluded that structural diversity is insufficient to enhance learning, it is necessary to create the diverse interpersonal interactions necessary for learning.
- Study and improve campus climates. One must feel safe in order to learn and grow.
- Advocate for social justice course work. If social justice courses are not currently available, advocate for their development; if courses exist, encourage students to enroll in them. Nothing indicates institutional support on a college campus more than inclusion in the curriculum as a for-credit course.
- Advocate for inclusion of social justice issues across the curriculum and cocurriculum. Specific social justice courses are not enough; a social justice perspective should permeate the campus climate.
- Work to change unjust policies, practices, and laws. Identify where groups are treated unjustly (for example, lack of partner benefits for lesbian and gay employees), and lobby for change. Expand your influence beyond campus to local, state, and federal governments.
- Know and use institutional decision-making structures strategically (von Destinon, Evans, and Wall, 2000). Student and faculty groups often have considerable power to enact change and can serve as partners in change.
- Frequent institutions that support justice; boycott institutions that do not. Educate others about both types of institutions.
- Persevere. Institutional change occurs slowly, but that must not dissuade action.

Supporting Target Group Members. While student affairs professionals can provide support to large groups of target group members through their work on policy issues, it is important also to provide one-on-one support, witness, and advocacy. This is not a call to do for students or other target group members what they should be doing for themselves. Rather, in social contexts where target group members are denied access to resources and social power, allies sometimes are able to use their greater social power to call attention to injustice. In addition, allies can provide support by being witnesses to the experiences of target group members. Often target group members' experiences are rendered invisible, misconstrued, or ignored by society as a whole. Accurately witnessing and listening can be a powerful mechanism of support:

- Listen. Do not assume you are an expert (Kivel, 2002). No matter how long you have been an ally, you have much to learn from members of target groups.
- Diversify your friendship group. Make a point to develop relationships with people who are visibly (and invisibly) different from you. Then be a friend.
- Be visible in your support, being careful that your visibility does not take attention away from target group members. Be visible to and with target group members, not in lieu of them.
- Educate yourself so that you can effectively provide support to target group members. Know the history of target group members, as well as institutional, local, and national resources available to assist and support them.
- Do not expect praise. Target group members may be ambivalent about your support at first (Bishop, 2002).
- Apologize when necessary (von Destinon, Evans, and Wall, 2000). Allies make mistakes; effective allies recognize their mistakes, apologize, and learn from them.
- Persevere. Giving up when the situation becomes difficult sends a message to target group members and reinforces a sense of distrust between groups.

Difficulties and Obstacles

"Do something" is a common refrain when encouraging social justice allies. Taking action obviously is a requisite for allies. We recognize, however, that such advice is often easier said than done. An ally identity is a difficult identity to maintain; one need only refer to the biographies of social justice allies to confirm this. Stokes Brown (2002), for example, outlines the losses associated with social justice work for four prominent racial justice allies, including exile from friends and family, loss of income, and imprisonment. Stokes Brown's social justice allies overcame these obstacles and persevered, but not without struggle and commitment.

Allies negotiate and balance multiple social group memberships with isolation and segregation. They have the privileges of dominant group membership but may be ostracized from the dominant group because of their work on behalf of target groups. Allies often are called "divisive" (Johnson, 2000) or "traitorous" (Bailey, 1998), or they are accused of exacerbating differences and ignoring commonalities (Levine and Cureton, 1998). White or male allies, for example, may even welcome the label of traitor, but must also recognize they cannot ever fully avoid the privileges associated with whiteness or maleness in our society.

Allies are not part of the target group either. Those who attempt to claim target group membership risk being counterproductive, often usurping the voice of target group members. Bishop (2002) wrote of a young man at a rally to memorialize female victims of domestic violence, who assumed an inappropriate level of membership in the women's movement. She wrote how the young man's intrusion onto the program of the rally, presumably to show support and solidarity, produced feelings of fear, insecurity, and helplessness in many of the women present at the rally. Bishop's is a vivid and powerful example of the negative consequences of co-opting group membership. Unfortunately, the balance between supporting and co-opting is not clearly delineated in most instances and must be negotiated by individual allies within the context of social movements.

Renouncing privilege and being ostracized by dominant group members, while purposefully not claiming target group status, may leave allies feeling detached and alone. Throughout this volume, the authors have encouraged allies to find like-minded peers for support. A formal group of like-minded allies also constitutes a powerful influence for social justice on campus. Ally groups support the efforts of target groups, initiate programming, offer visible and institutionalized support, and provide training and modeling for developing social justice allies.

Being an ally is difficult and often requires sacrifice, which makes maintaining motivation equally difficult. It becomes imperative that allies do not quit once a visible role in the justice movement is assumed. Allies who lack the constitution to continue once the work becomes difficult or the sacrifices too great often do more harm than good. Doing nothing is sometimes better than starting a task that goes unfinished (Bishop, 2002). A fair-weather ally, who works only when it is convenient or easy, risks reinforcing the suspicions of target group members through more unfulfilled promises.

Finally, allies need to be gentle and forgiving of themselves, as well as others. Dass and Gorman (1985), in writing about social justice work, asked, "If we are not rooted in compassion, how will our acts contribute to a compassionate world?" (p. 165). That compassion must include people we are working to support, people we are hoping will join us in ally work, and ourselves. Social justice advocacy can be difficult and draining work, although also often fulfilling and sustaining. It is inevitable that engaged allies will make mistakes, miss opportunities to intervene, and on occasion act in ways incongruent with their values. Mistakes and shortcomings need to be addressed, but we must also recognize that they are inevitable parts of the learning process and that we are transformed as much by our work as is the world we seek to transform. Martin Luther King Jr. (1958) spoke of this in the context of nonviolence, saying, "It first does something to the hearts and souls of those committed to it. It gives them a new self-respect; it calls up resources of strength and courage that they did not know they had" (p. 219).

Finding Your Place at the Table

As the four editors met to plan this volume, our conversation quickly turned to our own social group identities (dominant and target) and our roles as social justice advocates; specifically, we attempted to answer, "What right do we have to do this work?" We began to employ the metaphor of a place at the table as we worked through this conversation. As we stated in the Editors' Notes, allies must find a precarious balance between knowing when to take a seat at the table of social justice advocacy, joining those who are oppressed at combating oppression; when to speak up; when to be silent in order to listen to the experiences of others; and when to leave the table altogether, so as not to infringe on or usurp the role of target group members in advocating for their own liberation. This chapter is meant to help allies find that balance—their place at the table.

The work of social justice is too important to ignore or abandon because of the precariousness of the ally identity. We agree with Johnson (2000): "As long as we participate in a society that transforms difference into privilege, there is no neutral ground to stand on" (p. 131). Allies play a vital role in social movements. Little will change until those in power recognize the injustice and begin to fight against the structures that maintain their power. Through our work in helping students develop as allies and in our own ally work, we move forward in that struggle.

References

Bailey, A. "Locating Traitorous Identities: Toward a View of Privilege-Cognizant White Character." *Hypatia*, 1998, *13*(3), 27–43.

Bishop, A. *Becoming an Ally: Breaking the Cycle of Oppression in People.* (2nd ed.) Halifax, Nova Scotia: Fernwood, 2002.

Bowser, B. P., and Hunt, R. G. (eds.). *Impacts of Racism on White Americans.* (2nd ed.) Thousand Oaks, Calif.: Sage, 1996.

Broido, E. M. "The Development of Social Justice Allies During College: A Phenomenological Investigation." *Journal of College Student Development*, 2000a, *41*, 3–18.

Broido, E. M. "Ways of Being an Ally to Lesbian, Gay, and Bisexual Students." In V. A. Wall and N. J. Evans (eds.), *Toward Acceptance: Sexual Orientation Issues on Campus.* Lanham, Md.: University Press of America, 2000b.

Dass, R., and Gorman. P. *How Can I Help?* New York: Knopf, 1985.

Evans, N. J., and Reason, R. D. "Guiding Principles: A Review and Analysis of Student Affairs Philosophical Statements." *Journal of College Student Development,* 2001, *42,* 359–377.

Howard, G. R. *We Can't Teach What We Don't Know: White Teachers, Multiracial Schools.* New York: Teachers College Press, 1999.

Johnson, A. *Privilege, Power, and Difference.* New York: McGraw-Hill, 2000.

King, M. L., Jr. *Stride Toward Freedom: The Montgomery Story.* New York: HarperCollins, 1958.

Kivel, P. *Uprooting Racism: How White People Can Work for Racial Justice.* (Rev. ed.) Gabriola Island, B.C., Canada: New Society Publishers, 2002.

Levine, A., and Cureton, J. S. *When Hope and Fear Collide: A Portrait of Today's College.* San Francisco: Jossey-Bass. 1998.

MacKinnon, F.J.D., Broido, E. M., and Wilson, M. E. "Issues in Student Affairs." In F.J.D. MacKinnon (ed.), *Rentz's Student Affairs Practice in Higher Education.* (3rd ed.) Springfield, Ill.: Charles C. Thomas, 2004.

Reason, R. D., Roosa Millar, E. A., and Scales, T. C. "Toward a Model of Interracial Social Justice Ally Development." Paper presented at the annual conference of the Association for the Study of Higher Education, Kansas City, Mo., Nov. 2004.

Stokes Brown, C. *Refusing Racism: White Allies and the Struggle for Civil Rights.* New York: Teachers College Press, 2002.

Tatum, B. D. *"Why Are All the Black Kids Sitting Together in the Cafeteria?" and Other Conversations About Race.* New York: Basic Books, 2003.

von Destinon, M., Evans, N. J., and Wall, V. A. "Navigating the Minefield: Sexual Orientation Issues and Campus Politics." In V. A. Wall and N. J. Evans (eds.), *Toward Acceptance: Sexual Orientation Issues on Campus.* Lanham, Md.: University Press of America, 2000.

ROBERT D. REASON *is assistant professor of education and professor-in-charge of the college student affairs program at Penn State University. He is also a research associate in Penn State's Center for the Study of Higher Education.*

ELLEN M. BROIDO *is assistant professor of higher education and student affairs at Bowling Green State University in Ohio.*

INDEX

Back Issue/Subscription Order Form

Copy or detach and send to:

Jossey-Bass, A Wiley Imprint, 989 Market Street, San Francisco CA, 94103-1741

Call or fax toll-free: Phone 888-378-2537 6:30AM – 3PM PST; Fax 888-481-2665

Back Issues: Please send me the following issues at $27 each
(Important: Please include ISBN number with your order.)

_____

_____

_____

$ _____   Total for single issues

$ _____   SHIPPING CHARGES: SURFACE   Domestic Canadian
                                     First Item $5.00 $6.00
                                     Each Add'l Item $3.00 $1.50
                 For next-day and second-day delivery rates, call the number listed above.

Subscriptions   Please __ start __ renew my subscription to *New Directions for Student Services* for the year 2_____at the following rate:

U.S.	__ Individual $75	__ Institutional $170
Canada	__ Individual $75	__ Institutional $210
All Others	__ Individual $99	__ Institutional $244

**For more information about online subscriptions visit
www.wileyinterscience.com**

$ Total single issues and subscriptions (Add appropriate sales tax
     for your state for single issue orders. No sales tax for U.S.
_____ subscriptions. Canadian residents, add GST for subscriptions and
     single issues.)

__Payment enclosed (U.S. check or money order only)

__VISA __ MC __ AmEx Card #_____Exp. Date_____

Signature ——————————————————————— Day Phone ——————————

__Bill Me (U.S. institutional orders only. Purchase order required.)

Purchase order # ————————————————————————————————
                 Federal Tax ID13559302   **GST 89102 8052**

Name _____

Address _____

_____

Phone _____ E-mail _____

For more information about Jossey-Bass, visit our Web site at www.josseybass.com

examines the influence of the Latino family, socioeconomic levels, cultural barriers, and other factors to understand the challenges faced by Latinos. Discusses administration, student groups, community colleges, support programs, cultural identity, Hispanic-Serving Institutions, and more. ISBN: 0-7879-7479-X

SS104   **Meeting the Needs of African American Women**
Mary F. Howard-Hamilton
Identifies and explores the critical needs for African American women as students, faculty, and administrators. This volume introduces theoretical frameworks and practical applications for addressing challenges; discusses identity and spirituality; explores the importance of programming support in recruitment and retention; describes the benefits of mentoring; and provides illuminating case studies of black women's issues in higher education. ISBN: 0-7879-7280-0

SS103   **Contemporary Financial Issues in Student Affairs**
John H. Schuh
This volume addresses the challenging financial situation facing higher education and offers creative solutions for student affairs staff. Topics include the differences between public and private institutions in funding student activities, how to demonstrate financial accountability to stakeholders, plus ways to address budget challenges in student unions, health centers, campus recreation, counseling centers, and student housing. ISBN: 0-7879-7173-1

SS102   **Meeting the Special Needs of Adult Students**
Deborah Kilgore, Penny J. Rice
This volume examines the ways student services professionals can best help adult learners. Chapters highlight the specific challenges that adult enrollment brings to traditional four-year and postgraduate institutions, which are often focused on the traditional-aged student experience. Explaining that adult students are typically involved in campus life in different ways than younger students are, the volume provides student services professionals with good guidance on serving an ever-growing population. ISBN: 0-7879-6991-5

SS101   **Planning and Achieving Successful Student Affairs Facilities Projects**
Jerry Price
Provides student affairs professionals with an examination of critical facilities issues by exploring the experiences of their colleagues. Illustrates that students' educational experiences are affected by residence halls, student unions, dining services, recreation and wellness centers, and campus grounds, and that student affairs professionals make valuable contributions to the success of campus facility projects. Covers planning, budgeting, collaboration, and communication through case studies and lessons learned. ISBN: 0-7879-6847-1

SS100   **Student Affairs and External Relations**
Mary Beth Snyder
Building positive relations with external constituents is as important in student affairs work as it is in any other university or college division. This issue is a long-overdue resource of ideas, strategies, and information aimed

at making student affairs leaders more effective in their interactions with important off-campus partners, supporters, and agencies. Chapter authors explore the current challenges facing the student services profession as well as the emerging opportunities worthy of student affairs interest.
ISBN: 0-7879-6342-9

SS99   **Addressing Contemporary Campus Safety Issues**
Christine K. Wilkinson, James A. Rund
Provided for practitioners as a resource book for both historical and evolving issues, this guide covers hazing, parental partnerships, and collaborative relationships between universities and the neighboring community. Addressing a new definition of a safe campus environment, the editors have identified topics such as the growth in study abroad, the implications of increased usage of technology on campus, and campus response to September 11. In addition, large-scale crisis responses to student riots and multiple campus tragedies have been described in case studies. The issue speaks to a more contemporary definition of a safe campus environment that addresses not only physical safety issues but also those of a psychological nature, a more diverse student body, and quality of life.
ISBN: 0-7879-6341-0

SS98   **The Art and Practical Wisdom of Student Affairs Leadership**
Jon Dalton, Marguerite McClinton
This issue collects reflections, stories, and advice about the art and practice of student affairs leadership. Ten senior student affairs leaders were asked to maintain a journal and record their personal reflections on practical wisdom they have gained in the profession. The authors looked inside themselves to provide personal and candid insight into the convictions and values that have guided them in their work and lives.
ISBN: 0-7879-6340-2

SS97   **Working with Asian American College Students**
Marylu K. McEwen, Corinne Maekawa Kodama, Alvin N. Alvarez, Sunny Lee, Christopher T. H. Liang
Highlights the diversity of Asian American college students, analyzes the "model minority" myth and the stereotype of the "perfidious foreigner," and points out the need to consider the racial identity and racial consciousness of Asian American students. Various authors propose a model of Asian American student development, address issues of Asian Americans who are at educational risk, discuss the importance of integration and collaboration between student affairs and Asian American studies programs, and offer strategies for developing socially conscious Asian American student leaders.
ISBN: 0-7879-6292-9S

**NEW DIRECTIONS FOR STUDENT SERVICES
IS NOW AVAILABLE ONLINE AT WILEY INTERSCIENCE**

What is Wiley InterScience?

Wiley InterScience is the dynamic online content service from John Wiley & Sons delivering the full text of over 300 leading scientific, technical, medical, and professional journals, plus major reference works, the acclaimed *Current Protocols* laboratory manuals, and even the full text of select Wiley print books online.

What are some special features of Wiley InterScience?

Wiley InterScience Alerts is a service that delivers table of contents via e-mail for any journal available on Wiley InterScience as soon as a new issue is published online.
Early View is Wiley's exclusive service presenting individual articles online as soon as they are ready, even before the release of the compiled print issue. These articles are complete, peer-reviewed, and citable.
CrossRef is the innovative multi-publisher reference linking system enabling readers to move seamlessly from a reference in a journal article to the cited publication, typically located on a different server and published by a different publisher.

How can I access Wiley InterScience?

Visit http://www.interscience.wiley.com

Guest Users can browse Wiley InterScience for unrestricted access to journal Tables of Contents and Article Abstracts, or use the powerful search engine.
Registered Users are provided with a *Personal Home Page* to store and manage customized alerts, searches, and links to favorite journals and articles. Additionally, Registered Users can view free Online Sample Issues and preview selected material from major reference works.
Licensed Customers are entitled to access full-text journal articles in PDF, with select journals also offering full-text HTML.

How do I become an Authorized User?

Authorized Users are individuals authorized by a paying Customer to have access to the journals in Wiley InterScience. For example, a university that subscribes to Wiley journals is considered to be the Customer. Faculty, staff and students authorized by the university to have access to those journals in Wiley InterScience are Authorized Users. Users should contact their Library for information on which Wiley journals they have access to in Wiley InterScience.

ASK YOUR INSTITUTION ABOUT WILEY INTERSCIENCE TODAY!